UNBROKEN

A book read by a thousand different people is a thousand different books.

– Andrei Tarkovsky

UNBROKEN

A Journey from Silence to Strength

— SUSHMITHA MADHUKAR —

This book has been published with all efforts taken to make the material error-free after the consent of the author. However, the author and the publisher do not assume and hereby disclaim any liability to any party for any loss, damage, or disruption caused by errors or omissions, whether such errors or omissions result from negligence, accident, or any other cause.

While every effort has been made to avoid any mistake or omission, this publication is being sold on the condition and understanding that neither the author nor the publishers or printers would be liable in any manner to any person by reason of any mistake or omission in this publication or for any action taken or omitted to be taken or advice rendered or accepted on the basis of this work. For any defect in printing or binding the publishers will be liable only to replace the defective copy by another copy of this work then available.

To my sister, Carrie.

You are a gift from God. Thank you for being my light and
gently bringing mine back when I had forgotten how to shine.

To my children, Avyan & Smyan.

You are my heart, my purpose, and my greatest joy. Without you,
nothing in this world would hold meaning. You are living proof that
prayers are answered, and that love can be reborn in the purest form.

To my love, Madhu.

Thank you for being my strength and my constant. I'm endlessly
grateful to walk this life with you.

To all the kind strangers in this book.

For every gesture of warmth, every word that lifted me, every small act that
carried significant meaning—you may never know what you gave me.
But I do. This book is for you.

Contents

Part B

CONTENTS

Prologue

My name is Sushmitha, but you can call me Sush, like sushi without the "i." To those who've known me most deeply, I'm Minnu—a name gently spoken into existence by my aunt moments after I was born. It's the name of home, of family, different from the formal one used by teachers and strangers.

This isn't the tale of an extraordinary life. It's the story of what light can do when it finds the darkest corners. Of what's possible when all seems lost, something stirs inside that says: begin again.

It's a story of resilience. Of strangers who showed unexpected kindness. Of hope that flickered even when the wind howled the hardest. And yes, it's a story with a happy ending—for happy endings motivate us to live, and the world needs more of them.

Where I stand today once felt unreachable. The path I took to get here still echoes with pain. But happy endings matter. They remind us to keep believing, to trust that even in the heaviest seasons of life, something good may still be waiting.

Today, I am a mother to twin boys who fill my home with laughter and light. A daughter my parents are proud of. A wife to a man whose love has steadied me, and a friend to those who've walked beside me.

Professionally, I lead teams that develop life-saving medicines for children with cancer and chronic illness. I've also founded a nonprofit to support education and care for those often overlooked—children in need and elderly souls without families. These are the ways I give back, the ways I honor those who once reached out to me.

But the journey here was steep. There were times I felt invisible. Times I was hungry, hurt, and utterly alone. I knew what it meant to feel unwanted. To carry burdens too heavy for a child. And yet, through it all, I was met by small mercies—glimpses of grace from people who didn't owe me anything, but offered something anyway.

This book is about what it means to rise—to choose compassion over resentment, grace over bitterness, and to let your heart stay soft even when the world tries to harden it.

In my loneliest moments, I could have turned to anything for comfort—many do—but I chose education. That choice—my quiet rebellion—became the ladder out of darkness. What we reach for in our pain shapes who we become.

I hope my story reminds you that healing is possible. That strength often grows in silence. That love—no matter how imperfect—can change a life. That being the light in someone's life may not fix everything, but it can mean everything.

This is my story. Thank you for opening your heart to it.

Let's begin.

Author's Disclaimer

This memoir reflects my experiences, emotions, and perspectives as I lived and understood them. While I have tried to recount events truthfully, memory is imperfect, and perspectives differ. The people in this book are portrayed as I experienced them, but their recollections and feelings may vary.

I intend not to misrepresent or place blame but to share my journey with honesty and vulnerability. Names and specific details have been changed to respect privacy. This story is mine, but I acknowledge that every person involved has their version of events.

Above all, this book is about healing, growth, and understanding. It is not meant to harm, but to shed light on the complexities of human relationships and resilience.

The World I Knew

I grew up in a small village in South India during the 90s—when villages still felt like villages. Life moved slower, more gently, untouched by the rush of highways or the glare of smartphone screens. The air was cleaner, calmer, and kinder. The scent of wet earth and woodsmoke lingered long after the sun rose. Roads weren't yet rivers of cars and honking horns; they were pathways shared by bicycles, bullock carts, and the occasional rickshaw carrying women, elders, and children wrapped in conversation and the rustling of saris.

Mornings held a kind of hush. Not silence, but a symphony of small, familiar sounds. The milkman's bicycle rattled down the narrow lanes, aluminum cans clinking against one another like a casual rhythm section. He called out softly, a practiced tone that stirred sleepy households awake.

Temple bells rang in the distance, their echoes mingling with the strains of Suprabhatam from someone's old radio. The call to Namaz rose in peaceful harmony somewhere not too far away. A rooster crowed, as punctual and persistent as ever. No alarms were needed—nature handled timekeeping just fine.

The houses along the street wore their age with pride. Some were painted in gentle pastels—faded blues and greens, soft yellows, and pinks, washed out by the sun and monsoon. Others stood bare, with whitewashed walls and freshly watered Tulasi plants at their doors. Rangolis greeted the dawn—vivid, imperfect, and already smudged by a stray cow or an excited child's footstep.

My parents arrived in this village with little more than hope in their hands. They were young, determined, and eager for a better life.

We lived in a small, modest rental—a two-room portion nestled beneath a thatched roof woven from palm leaves that whispered with every passing breeze. The house was simple, yet to us, it had everything. The roof allowed little slivers of sunlight to filter through during the day, and at night, it carried the lullabies of rustling leaves and distant crickets.

Our home wasn't grand. It had one multipurpose room that transformed into whatever we needed: a bedroom at night, a living room by day, a dining space when food was ready, and a guest room whenever someone dropped by. In one corner, clinging like a shy secret, was a tiny kitchen—barely large enough for two feet to stand in. But it featured a long gas stove that Mummy took great pride in.

We didn't own much: a single bed shared between us, a small stack of utensils, carefully folded clothes and a black-and-white television that sat in the corner like a prized possession. Four wooden shelves lined one wall, holding everything we needed—and somehow, it never felt like we lacked anything. To me, it was no less than a palace.

The veranda was my favorite place in the world. It was our front room, waiting room, cinema, and stage. Daddy often sat there, reading the newspaper, chatting with neighbors, or watching the world go by. On Sundays, we all gathered to watch old movies under the stars, huddling around the flickering screen of our little TV. I'd also do my homework there, surrounded by the everyday hum of village life—the creak of bicycles, the calls of vendors, and the distant bark of a dog.

Just beyond the veranda was a small patch of garden, shy and unkempt, stretching toward a timeworn wall. A drumstick tree stood guard there, tall and generous. I used to run my fingers along the wall's rough surface, imagining all the years it had witnessed, all the stories it had stored away in its cracks.

Beyond that wall, the world seemed vast and mysterious—but I never yearned for it. With its rustling roof and quiet comforts, that house was my entire universe. In that small world, we lived with more heart than a mansion could ever hold.

My mother—Mummy—was the quiet force that held our world together. Tall and fair, she moved through life wrapped in practical silk sarees—always chosen for their easy maintenance and modest price. She wasn't the overly affectionate kind of mother you read about or saw in films. There were no bedtime kisses or soft indulgences. Her love didn't come in hugs or lullabies—it came in discipline, drive, and relentless presence.

She was one of three children born into scarcity. Her father, my grandfather, worked as an electrician at a nearby sugar factory. The family lived in modest company quarters—a perk of the job but far from luxury. With a limited income, he not only raised his children, but also shouldered the responsibilities of his extended family. Being the eldest of seven siblings meant helping with everything from school fees to weddings to hospital visits. My grandmother stayed home, stretching every rupee to feed, clothe, and care for the family.

That was the world Mummy grew up in—where there was never quite enough: not enough food, not enough security, not enough room to dream.

So, when she married Daddy, she brought with her very little except a fierce, unbending will to create a better life than the one she'd known. Unlike many women of her time, she refused to stay at home. With minimal formal education, she found work as a teacher at a private school, teaching lower grades for a salary that barely counted—but to her, it meant dignity. It meant progress. Even the smallest income, she believed, could shift the weight of our future.

She taught in the very same school I attended. On days when I was sick, she still brought me along to school—armed with medicines and fluids in a bag, checking on me between classes. Her presence was constant. Watchful. She didn't miss a beat—not a low mark, wrong word, or misstep. And in that rhythm of her life, Daddy played his quiet part. While she worked, he cooked, helped care for me, and ran the home alongside her—a calm defiance of the gender roles that weighed down so many other families around us.

We didn't have much, but Mummy made sure we never looked like we had less. She saved for my clothes, tucked away bits of money to buy me tiny pieces of jewelry, and ensured that whatever I needed, I had. Not what I wanted—but always what I needed.

School wasn't a choice. It was a contract. My success was her mission. I studied, not out of joy, but out of duty—because her pride was stitched into my report cards. "Education is your ticket," she'd say, voice stern. "You suffer now; you smile later." That was her promise, not of comfort but of purpose.

I didn't make it easy either. I was mischievous, wild with my friends, and quick to lie when I felt cornered. But lying wasn't rebellion—it was self-preservation. Telling the truth to Mummy felt like stepping into a storm. There was no space for softness in her justice—only the thunder of disappointment. I wasn't afraid of punishment. I was scared of letting her down. At the time, her love felt suffocating. Her rules, expectations, and relentless watchfulness felt like a weight. But with time, I've come to see it.

She was seventeen when I was born—a child raising a child. She didn't enter motherhood with a blueprint for warmth. Instead, she carried a memory of what it felt like to be overlooked, and she swore I'd never feel the same. She wasn't trying to be gentle; she was trying to save me.

Daddy's story, like Mummy's, began simply, but it carried a different weight. He was the son of farmers, one of four children, and the undisputed apple of my grandmother's eye. He grew up with no shortage of food on the table—home-cooked meals fresh from the fields—but dreams and discipline were in shorter supply. Education was never the priority it should have been. He failed grades, repeated a few, and eventually left school without finishing his degree.

With no financial cushion or family inheritance and a young wife and daughter to care for, he carved his path the only way he knew how: with quiet perseverance. He moved a few kilometers away from the village in which he was born and became a government contractor, working on roads and buildings—creating infrastructure in a village that is taking its steps to become a town.

If Mummy ruled the house with sharp corners and precise lines, Daddy was the soft light filling the rest. He was funny, gentle, and easy in a way few adults ever are. While Mummy stood for structure, he gave me space. He was my best friend before I even knew what that meant. He corrected me without scolding, forgave me without fanfare, and always protected me from Mummy's strictness.

As a child, I used to imagine I was born only to him—not to Mummy. I couldn't fathom that a man who made up silly songs on his Vespa, who tickled me into fits of laughter, wasn't the one who brought me into this world. Biology didn't matter. With him, I felt chosen and loved without condition.

Whenever the pressure of school or expectations became too much, he'd whisk me away on his old second-hand Vespa. The wind would tug at my hair, and he'd hum nonsensical tunes, singing about trees that walked or cows that danced. I'd laugh until my stomach ached, my troubles left behind like dust. Those rides were our little escape—a world where nothing mattered but the road, the breeze, and the joy between us.

At night, I slept beside him, curled into his warmth. He lay between me and Mummy like a shield. Not from monsters or nightmares—but from the only thing that truly scared me then: Mummy. With Daddy beside me, I felt safe, guarded, and understood. He didn't question my fears; he just stayed close.

He didn't push me to be extraordinary. He didn't demand straight A's or perfect manners. All he wanted was for me to be okay, happy, and maybe to laugh with him a little longer.

Looking back now, I see that while Mummy gave me strength, Daddy gave me softness. She taught me how to survive; he taught me how to breathe. Between the two of them, I grew.

Sundays were sacred—not for the rituals or the rest, but for the journeys they promised—to the two homes that made me feel most loved and most myself.

My maternal grandparents' house lay just a few kilometers away, a short ride on Daddy's bike. But every time we turned onto their street, it felt like entering a different universe—one scented forever with Ammamma's chicken curry. That smell—fiery, familiar, and comforting—greeted me like a long-lost friend. Ammamma would be busy at the stove, calling me between stirs, while my grandfather sat cross-legged in his spot, waiting.

He'd lost his teeth in an accident but not his spirit. He taught me the perfect ratio of curry to rice, showing me how to squish it with just the right amount of ghee. We never needed words. His eyes sparkled with mischief, and I knew a movie outing was coming when he winked. I'd hop onto the little bar in front of his creaky bicycle, and off we'd go—to dusty theaters or crowded markets. I was his movie buddy, his errand partner, his little sidekick.

Their love for each other wasn't poetic or picture-perfect. They bickered, nagged, and yelled. But beneath it all was something steady: their love for me. Even as a child, I felt that constant hum of affection that needed no performance.

At my paternal grandparents' home, life moved slower, quieter, and sacred in a different way. Nanamma, my paternal grandmother, was small, dark from sun and soil, always up before dawn. The sound of her mantras whispered through the soft ring of a bell, would float through the house like a blessing. After her prayers, she'd gently press sweet Prashad into my palm—warm, soft, and sacred. I'd cup it like treasure, not because of its taste but because it came from her hands.

That house smelled of cows and wet earth—milk boiled on the stove in the early light. The walls were rough, plastered unevenly, and often chipped—but it never felt like anything was missing. My grandfather, silent and kind, would walk me to the nearby store each morning for rations. Every time, without fail, he'd slip me a few peppermint tablets on the way back. He never said why; he didn't have to. His smile was enough.

Their home wasn't polished or loud. There were no grand meals or outings. But there was peace—quiet, grounding peace that settled into my bones like a warm sun. That simplicity, that slow rhythm, held a kind of wholeness that Mummy's driven world couldn't offer. I didn't need to be good, thoughtful, or careful in that house. I just needed to be.

Two houses. Two sets of grandparents. Two different kinds of love. And me, the lucky child who belonged to both.

But love, at home with Mummy, looked different. It was sharp-edged and urgent, wrapped in ambition and fierce determination. She left no stone unturned in shaping my future. School, dance, singing, karate, and eight years of Hindi lessons provided me with plans and backup plans. If higher education failed, she envisioned me teaching Hindi in a government job with stability and a secure future.

There was no room for failure. Mistakes weren't tolerated. Tears were seen as a weakness. Success was the only option.

I struggled to accept that it was love—relentless and consuming, but love, nonetheless. But sometimes, the people around us see what we cannot.

We shared the house with two other families. In one portion, a quiet man lived with his elderly mother, drawing cartoons for the local paper. On the other, a Muslim couple raised their two kids, whose laughter rang through the courtyard while I sat sulking in front of my books.

One afternoon, the artist called us three children over. His room smelled of pencil shavings and old paper. He handed each of us a sketch. The siblings received drawings of children running, faces full of joy. "Mine was a little girl with pigtails.

She wasn't running or laughing.

Her mother was hitting her."

That's how he saw it—how some others might have. What I perceived as discipline and devotion, he drew as pain. As violence.

I didn't see the message. I only saw the pigtails, the familiar shape of my frame. I smiled. I liked it. I ran home to show Mummy. Her face changed. She took the drawing without a word. I never saw it again.

Whatever I became, she had sown the seeds—unapologetically, in her way. She refused to let me settle. Her love was armor, not warmth. But it held me all the same.

I thought this life, this house, this family, this village—was all there would ever be.

Until one day, I overheard a conversation in the kitchen.

"Adoption." "America."

My heart thudded.

I told myself it meant nothing. Just talk—just words.

My life was here—in the soil, jasmine, Daddy's laughter, and Ammamma's curry.

Nothing could change that.

Or so I thought.

"Remember, some things have to end for better things to begin."

The Plan

Years passed in a familiar loop—school days under Mummy's watchful eye, evenings filled with extracurriculars, and summers that revolved around the constant orbit of my grandparents' home. That was the universe I knew: predictable, tightly held, and impossibly small.

The summers of my childhood felt simpler, softer, and endlessly warm. Mummy, my aunt, her two sons, and I journeyed to my grandparents' house each year. The dads visited only occasionally. Without them, it was seven of us who crammed into that small home. The walls stretched just enough to hold us all—but even they had their limits. When the house couldn't keep us, and the summer heat pressed in too thick to bear, we spilled out into the open—into the yard shaded by neem trees, under a sky heavy with stars. We didn't have designated beds; we lay wherever there was space each night. But when Daddy came, he was given a bed.

Our bed was nothing more than a small cot, barely big enough for one. He shared it with me. It was cramped, but I didn't care. I'd curl into him, half my body draped over his, my head resting on his chest, rising and falling with his breath. We talked for hours—about everything and nothing. The stars above. The movies we loved. His voice was steady and low, wrapping around me like a lullaby. And as the night deepened, the world faded, the stars blurred, and I'd drift off to sleep, safe in the warmth of his arms.

By the time I woke up, he'd be gone back to our home. I wouldn't see him again for days.

The mornings brought their kind of thrill. Unlike our home, where each family had a bathroom, we shared common toilets a few yards away.

We carried our buckets in line, giggling with the other kids, already plotting our daily mischief.

By the time we returned, Ammamma was already in the kitchen, rushing to finish breakfast before my grandfather left for work at 7 a.m. His schedule set the tempo of the house. He'd eat, sip his coffee, and go. At noon, he returned for lunch, took a short nap, and returned to work by 1 p.m. At five, he was home again. Everything—meals, noise, movement—slowed or quickened around his presence.

But once he left, Ammamma was all ours.

Freed from her wifely duties, she poured herself into us. She made sure we were fed, cared for, and happy. We helped her roll dough into tiny balls for puris, giggling as they puffed up like golden balloons in hot oil. We devoured mangoes of every kind, fighting over the seed at the center, taking turns savoring its sweet, fibrous goodness. My grandparents didn't have store-bought toys or fancy treats—but they didn't need to. Their love was enough.

When the year-end report cards arrived, Mummy fretted over my 90% grades while my aunt celebrated my cousins' 60%. Puzzled by Mummy's worry, my grandparents assumed I had failed.

The days stretched long and golden, filled with laughter, races through the neighborhood, and games that only ended when the sun dipped below the horizon. Those summers were stitched together with love, simplicity, and vivid memories that lingered long after they finished.

And then, as always, summer ended.

We packed our bags and left the warm, chaotic embrace of my grandparents' home, returning to our tiny rental where school, homework, and quiet expectations awaited. Life slipped back into its familiar rhythm— but that year, something felt different. Something had shifted.

It began with the phone calls.

They came late at night when the rest of the house was quiet. We had just gotten a black rotary phone, its coiled cord stretching across the floor like a lifeline to someplace far beyond us. Heavy and humming with possibilities, it sat on a small table by the bed. And when it rang, Mummy always answered.

Her back was straight, her voice low but animated, and she spoke in hushed tones to her uncle—her father's younger brother—who had lived in the United States for as long as I could remember. Sometimes, the calls lasted thirty minutes; sometimes, more than an hour.

That's how *The Plan* began—quietly, subtly, like a thread weaving its way into the fabric of our lives before we even noticed it.

Her uncle's family had long since become American. U.S. citizens. That status carried weight in our world as if they had passed into some exclusive realm of success. I had met them during their visits to India, but the memories were fragmented and tinged with discomfort.

Whenever they came, they were treated like royalty. They brought gifts, spent easily, and stood apart—foreign yet still somehow ours. But I never felt at ease around them. One memory in particular stuck with me.

It was a family gathering. I was playing with their children—a girl about my age and a much younger boy. We ran through the house, laughing, caught in the wild, joyful chaos of childhood. Suddenly, the boy grabbed a bottle of red liquid bindi and smeared it into my eye.

Pain flared. I cried out, "It hurts! It hurts!" I ran to the nearest adult, tears streaming down my face. At first, they panicked, thinking it was blood. But when they realized it was just dye, their concern faded. There were no scoldings, no apologies. The boy laughed, delighted by my pain.

If I had done something like that, Mummy would have been furious. I would've been punished and taught a lesson. But his parents did nothing.

They watched, distant and unbothered. That's how I remembered them—detached, privileged, untouchable. And in that moment, I felt small.

I didn't know then that these very people would shape the course of my life.

As the phone calls stretched on, *The Plan* began to take shape—not all at once, but slowly, like an idea testing its weight in the air. At first, it was whispers, then words, then possibility.

At home, cracks had already begun to form.

Daddy's contracts and trucking business had always been unstable. Some months were good. Others, we scraped by. We managed, thanks to Mummy—her careful planning, her teacher's salary, and her unshakeable belief that discipline and hard work could keep chaos at bay. For a long time, she made it work.

But then came the oil contract.

It was supposed to be our turning point. Daddy sold his lorries—our main source of income at the time—to invest in something bigger. Mummy emptied her savings. She even gave up the few gold pieces she had collected over the years, piece by piece, with quiet pride. They bet everything.

And they lost everything.

The contract failed, and with it, the life they had fought so hard to build collapsed. They returned not just broke but broken. There was no home to return to—not the one they had sacrificed so much for. Their dreams vanished overnight, swallowed by a promise that never came through.

And so, *The Plan* stepped out of the shadows and into the center of our lives.

This was the plan: Mummy's uncle in the U.S. wanted to sponsor his brother in India—the one without children. The idea was that he would adopt me and another boy. Through that adoption, we'd apply for visas and, if all went well, move to America as a family.

The promise? A brighter future. A better life.

The proposal was both alluring and terrifying. If my parents agreed to give me up—legally—to her uncle, I would be taken to the U.S., given an education, and offered a life far beyond what they could afford. It was presented as an investment, a one-time sacrifice with long-term returns.

But the costs were ours to bear. No help from the sponsor. No help from the adoptive parents. Every legal fee, every travel expense, every document—it all fell on us. On my parents, who had nothing left to give.

And still, they agreed.

Because when all else was lost, this plan—however uncertain, however distant—was the only path that still glowed with possibility.

My parents didn't understand what life in America meant: the cost of living, the burden of education, and the emotional toll of giving your child away. Yet, in their eyes, America was salvation—success, stability, and escape all wrapped into one. It wasn't a matter of if it would work; it was a question of when. Even then, I don't think they truly believed it would happen, not deep down. It felt like a story you tell yourself in the dark, a fantasy, a desperate gamble. But still, they held onto it, just in case.

As the process moved forward, my biological household was split into "in favor" and "not in favor." My maternal grandfather was thrilled. To him, this was an investment—a chance to elevate the entire family's status. His faith in his brothers was unwavering, shaped by years of shared history; he believed in them. My paternal grandfather, however, was furious. He was a man of few words, but when he spoke, it mattered. His hearing had faded with age, so he relied on reading lips.

When Daddy approached his parents with the proposal, he turned first to my grandmother. "There's a plan to adopt Ammulu and take her to the U.S.," Daddy said.

My grandmother froze, her face unreadable.

My grandfather's expression darkened as he turned to Daddy, eyes steady. "What do you mean, adoption? She is your only child." His voice was firm, his disapproval absolute.

"If she wants to go to the U.S., let her study. Let her earn her way. But not like this." "Can you live without Minamma (a loving nickname given to me by my paternal family)?"

The discussion continued and ended with my grandpa saying his "not in favor."

Daddy, caught between these opposing forces, wrestled with doubt. However, if my parents argued, they did it in private. In front of me, they were united. Their faces were calm, their smiles forced but unwavering; they never let me see their struggle. And Mummy never asked me how I felt.

I wish she did. I wanted her to hold me, reassure me, and tell me I wasn't being sent away because I wasn't wanted but because she believed it was best for me. I wanted to hear that it hurt her too. But she never let me in. She made decisions in silence, her expression unreadable, as though sheer resolve could carry us through. I watched everything unfold quietly, knowing better than to question her. So, I pretended.

I pretended as if nothing was changing. As if I wasn't being handed over. As if the idea of leaving everything behind wasn't terrifying.

The phone calls continued. The paperwork piled up. The dream of America grew larger and closer.

The adoption process was surprisingly easy. While I was at school, both parents—biological and adoptive—went to a registration office. An hour later, it was done.

On paper, I had new parents. In my heart, nothing had changed. But in reality, everything had.

A decision was made: I would stay in the same school, continuing my education while living with Mummy and Daddy. My adoptive parents lived in a remote village, tending to a farm. The nearest school was five miles away, only reachable on foot. It wasn't practical for me to go with them.

But when Mummy's anger lashed out at me, I secretly longed to escape. I imagined my adoptive parents as my saviors—kind, patient, never saying no, letting me play for hours. In my mind, they were everything I needed. Yet the warmth I had dreamed of wasn't there when they visited. They weren't cold but weren't the loving figures I had built in my head.

I didn't start calling them "Mom" and "Dad". They were my parents now, but I still called them Grandma and Grandpa—our old relationship unchanged by legal papers.

At school, my last name changed. I now carried Mummy's maiden name, matching my adoptive parents. It wasn't unfamiliar, but it wasn't mine. No one said anything about it, but I felt the shift deep inside me.

As a child, you believe the world revolves around your worries. You imagine your internal turmoil spilling into your environment, reshaping everything in its path. So when my last name changed, I braced myself for a seismic shift at school—whispers in the hallways, lingering glances, questions from friends and teachers.

But nothing changed.

During roll call, they read out my new last name, and that was it. No one paused, no one looked up, and life moved forward, uninterrupted.

It was a quiet realization—people are too absorbed in their own worlds, busy navigating the storms in their own minds. What felt monumental to me was just another fleeting detail to everyone else.

I watched all of this silently because Mummy wouldn't tolerate any questions or concerns from me. She wouldn't even let me bring up the topic. Reflecting, I cannot fathom why she shut me out the way she did. I speak to my children, have conversations, and get their opinions on even the smallest decisions, like planning a playdate. But back then, Mummy planned and rewrote the course of my life without asking how I felt or reassuring me.

It was all happening to me, being done for me, but I wasn't allowed to feel, talk, or worry about it. I had to pretend nothing was changing, as if this plan wasn't insane. Life went on, but I knew something monumental was shifting. I didn't know how to process it or if I even could.

It felt less like a dream and more like a storm gathering on the horizon—one I couldn't see but could feel in the air, heavy and unavoidable. I felt like a helpless child bride, being given away just as my grandmothers were, as if it was normal as if this was how things were always done. Everyone around me acted as if this were just another rite of passage—except for me, the one being sent away.

In many Indian families, a daughter's wedding is more than just a celebration—a duty, a passage, a lifelong farewell wrapped in ritual and gold. Parents pour their fortunes into the wedding, ensuring their daughter leaves with dignity, and her future is handed to her husband and his family. Some daughters never truly return home; their visits are fleeting, and their ties stretch thin across miles and traditions. It is a responsibility taken with the utmost seriousness, a duty to be fulfilled no matter the cost.

Both my grandmothers were given away as brides when they were barely children—one at thirteen, the other at fourteen. Marriage was not just expected; it was inevitable. They became wives and mothers before they understood themselves, their childhoods traded for duty, and their innocence swallowed by expectation.

Perhaps that's why, when I was fourteen, my parents saw me as grown. They did everything parents of a bride would do—preparing, planning, letting go. But in my case, there was no groom. There was no wedding. Instead, there was adoption. I wasn't sent off to a husband's home, but to another family and life. The rituals were different, but the farewell was just as final.

"If it comes, take it. If it goes, let it."

The Interview

I had always been young for my class, requiring my parents to secure special permissions for me to sit for my 7th, 10th, and 11th-grade exams. I had just received my results for the eleventh grade and started my twelfth when the gears of our visa processing began to turn with newfound urgency.

The call came unexpectedly, as these things often do. We were summoned to the Chennai consulate once again for another interview. Over the years, I had attended a few interviews with my adoptive family, and at times, only my adoptive father had gone. Our visa had never been outright rejected before, but each visit ended with a request for more documents, more clarification—and more waiting.

But this time felt different. The consulate had asked that all four of us attend—my adoptive family and me. Mummy came along, too, and we stayed at my aunt's house in Chennai, a city that always felt overwhelming to me. The noise, the crowds, the suffocating heat was a world away from the slow, predictable rhythm of our Village.

Daddy didn't come. He had business to attend to, or at least that's what he said. But deep down, I wondered if it was easier for him to stay behind, to avoid confronting what was about to happen. Maybe if he didn't see me go, it wouldn't feel as real.

Despite everything, Mummy remained her usual self—stoic, unflinching, and seemingly unaffected. I observed her on the train, waiting for hesitation for the slightest crack in her resolve. But she never faltered. She spoke of the visa like it was just another milestone to cross, another step in the path she had laid out for me. She never acknowledged what it meant—I would soon no longer be hers.

On the train, I overheard the adults whispering, their voices low but heavy with certainty.

"This time, it'll go through," one said.

Things were looking positive, they all agreed.

Three months ago, another family—sponsored by Mummy's uncle—successfully obtained their visas. They had already left for the U.S., and their success felt like a promise that our turn was next.

Despite the hopeful whispers around me, I felt no excitement.

Even after legally becoming my adoptive parents' daughter, little changed. I still lived with Mummy and Daddy, attended the same school, and saw my adoptive family only a few times a year when they visited. At one time, they had longed for children, but now, in their fifties, I wasn't sure if they had the energy—or even the space in their lives—to fully step into that role. On paper, they had children. In reality, the bond remained distant.

They weren't particularly eager about moving to the U.S. either. If the visa was granted without a financial burden on them, they were willing to take that step. Perhaps, in their way, they saw it as fulfilling their duty, an opportunity to provide us with something better. But no one ever asked what it meant for me. No one looked beyond the visa, beyond the plane ticket. No one questioned whether this was truly a dream come true – or just the promise of something better without knowing what "better" meant.

The walk from the local train station to the consulate felt longer than it was, each step heavy with the weight of uncertainty. The path was lined with towering, well-aged trees, their branches stretching out like silent witnesses to the hopes and fears that passed beneath them. Families sat under their shade, fanning themselves, whispering quiet prayers, their eyes filled with longing and desperation. I took it all in—the hushed murmurs, the restless shifting, the unspoken worries—as I moved forward, my heart pounding with nervous anticipation.

As we approached the consulate for our interview, a long line of people stretched outside, their faces etched with anticipation.

The Chennai sun was beginning to hit its peak, burning hot in the mid-morning sky, but no one seemed to notice either the heat or the burn. Inside, they were already burning with anticipation and nervousness, their futures hanging in the balance of the next few hours. Students stood in line, hoping for a chance to further their education and improve their family's economic standing; parents yearning to visit their sons or daughters; fresh graduates eager to work in the U.S. and build their careers; and families like ours, hoping to move permanently in pursuit of the American Dream.

A security guard checked our paperwork before allowing us inside. Mummy and her cousin accompanied us to the interview, but they were not allowed inside the building. They stopped a few yards away while the security guard checked us in. I turned to look at her one last time before stepping inside the door, and I saw something in her eyes: a silent prayer, a quiet faith in my ability.

Inside, the consulate was cold and impersonal. Rows of chairs, harsh fluorescent lights, and glass windows showed visa officers sitting behind counters, calling up one applicant at a time. I scanned the room, my heart pounding.

Several windows processed different visa types—visitor, work, student—but only one was designated for immigrant visas. That was where our fate would be decided. We waited, the seconds stretching endlessly, until something unexpected happened.

A small window to the side that had remained closed suddenly slid open. A voice called my adoptive father's name.

We jumped to our feet, scrambling to gather our belongings. My adoptive father clutched the bulging blue folder—our entire lives crammed into a single binder—while I carried a bag filled with extra papers and a water bottle. We hurried toward the window, our steps quick and slightly unsteady.

The officer—a man of Indian origin—began the interview. He asked for some papers, and with the help of my adoptive father, I fished them out of the blue folder and presented them to him. My adoptive parents barely spoke English, and my adoptive sibling struggled as well, so it fell on me to answer.

Then, the officer looked directly at me.

"How many children do your biological parents have?"

I met his gaze, my pulse racing. "Just me. I'm an only child."

A pause.

"Why did they give you up for adoption if you're their only child?"

The question hit like a slap—sudden, intimate, and disorienting.

"They couldn't afford to raise even one child on their limited income," I said, the words sliding out like they belonged to someone else.

I spoke with a confidence that surprised even me as if I had rehearsed the answer many times—though I hadn't. But as I finished, something inside me cracked. Was that the truth? Or is it just the answer everyone needed me to believe?

One of my greatest strengths, which Mummy recognized and nurtured from an early age, was my speaking ability. Both my Nanamma and Daddy were exceptional orators—eloquent and commanding in front of any audience. It was a gift they passed down to me. Public speaking and communication became my strongest suit. I began addressing audiences as early as the third grade, and the first time I competed, I secured second place. From that moment on, I became a regular participant in school events, debate competitions, and public speaking opportunities, consistently earning first place.

Though I still felt nervous like my fellow participants before every speech, I learned to channel that fear into focus. I practiced relentlessly, honing my ability to project confidence in my words and delivery. That skill shaped my academic and personal growth and proved invaluable in unexpected ways. This confidence and clarity of speech helped me navigate the unforeseen questions during the visa interview. I answered on the spot, thinking quickly and with conviction.

The officer studied me for a moment before shifting his attention back to the documents. My adoptive father passed a few more papers through the window, and the officer flipped through them, scanning each page carefully.

The interview lasted about 30 minutes.

And then, with a simple nod, he said the words we had been waiting for.

"It's granted."

We didn't want to make a celebratory gesture as we were unsure if it was appropriate. We thanked the interviewer, gathered our papers, and walked toward the exit. We stepped outside, dazed. Mummy was waiting, her face anxious. The moment we told her the news, she hugged us all, and tears flowed.

In this entire journey—from hushed phone calls to legal paperwork to final approval—this was the very first time I saw her cry.

A part of me softened for a moment as if I had been holding my breath for years, waiting for this exact crack in her armor.

But another part of me wondered—why now?

Why not when they signed the adoption papers? Why not when my name changed? Why not when I silently begged her to ask how I felt?

Was this her way of saying goodbye?

Was it too late to stop now—even if she wanted to?

For a second, I wanted her to say, "Let's go home. We don't have to do this."

But she didn't.

So I swallowed everything and kept walking.

We took the local train back, talking over one another and reciting what happened at the consulate. By afternoon, we returned to my aunt's house, where the mood was celebratory. There was laughter, excitement, talk of packing, and travel dates. Everyone saw this as the happy ending.

After we reached my aunt's house, Mummy informed Daddy over the phone. He didn't speak to me, so I wasn't sure how he felt about it. I used to imagine that he was sad, that he couldn't sleep all night, thinking about not having me next to him as we slept.

But I couldn't shake the feeling deep in my chest – something cold, something uncertain.

I had heard whispers in the family about the sponsor with whom we would be staying—stories about how he treated his mother, how the wife and husband didn't get along, and how they were cruel to their previous guests. I had heard about another family who had stayed with them before and left broken and estranged.

Sometimes, the truth stands right before us, clear as day, yet we choose to look away. Not because we don't see it, but because accepting it would mean unraveling the comfort of our illusions.

Was I walking into something better? Or something far worse?

To my family, this was a miracle. In our village, only the wealthiest could dream of sending their children abroad. It was an impossible feat for those without land, assets, or financial stability. And yet, here I was—not even halfway through my education, preparing to board a plane to the U.S. with a green card status.

They called me lucky. Blessed. Fortunate beyond measure.

But as I sat among my family that night, listening to their eager conversations, I felt like a passenger on a journey I hadn't thoroughly chosen. The American Dream was within reach, but at what cost?

What was I about to gain?

What was I about to lose?

I didn't have the answers then. I wouldn't for a long time.

All I knew was that my life would change in ways I couldn't yet fathom. There was no turning back—only the unknown stretching before me, vast and uncertain.

And I had no choice but to walk into it.

"The right door, the door meant for you,
will open without knocking!"

The Journey Begins

The time had come.

The dream that had taken years to create was finally taking shape, yet it brought a whirlwind of uncertainty.

Even though the cost of getting me to the U.S. was only a fraction of what it could have been, it was still far beyond our means. My parents, who had already stretched every rupee to make ends meet, now had to find the funds for two plane tickets—one for me and one for one of my adoptive parents. His family would cover my adoptive sibling's ticket, who would also pay for the other adoptive parent's fare. We were spending money we didn't have, borrowing, scraping together every bit we could, and pouring everything into a future none of us could fully envision.

There was so much to do, so many details to arrange. My parents took me shopping for new clothes—pants, dresses, nightgowns—things I had never owned.

In our small village, clothes were stitched by the local tailor—a man who worked in a dimly lit shop, surrounded by fabric scraps and the rhythmic hum of his sewing machine. The pants were a little loose, the shirts too big, and their patterns were outdated before being worn. What mattered was durability, not style.

For nightwear, Mummy chose fabrics with different patterns—some covered in delicate flowers, others with bold symbols—and had them sewn to my measurements. Again, they were too big and too modest.

But stepping into the Western world, those clothes became a silent marker of difference—too bright, baggy, and unfamiliar. A single outfit could remind you that you didn't quite fit in in a place where belonging was dictated by the most minor details.

We packed suitcases filled with non-perishable food—200 pounds of lentils, spices, tamarind, sweets, pickles, turmeric, and chili powder. It wasn't just food; it was a way to ensure we wouldn't become a burden to the sponsor family, a way to carry home with me even as I left it behind.

Amidst all of this, I struggled with a mix of emotions. There was relief at moving away from Mummy's cold, distant presence but also grief. I knew I would miss Daddy, my grandparents, and my home.

If my parents felt sadness about sending me away, they continued to not show it.

But my grandparents didn't hide their sorrow. Nanamma was the unhappiest of all. She often told my birth story, a tale woven with faith and prophecy.

The night before I was born, she dreamed of the goddess Lakshmi cradling a baby girl.

"This child will be born into your home," the goddess had said. *"She will bring fortune and prosperity wherever she goes."*

Nanamma believed it with all her heart. She believed that I was Daddy's last stroke of good luck. And now, he was sending me away.

"This will not end well for him," she warned.

That story has always stayed with me, a quiet anchor in moments of doubt. Through countless challenges and uncertainties in the years that followed, I held on to the belief that I was born with a purpose, that I was meant to become something greater. When faced with hardships like poverty, I reminded myself that they were only temporary obstacles on the path to fulfilling the destiny my 'Nanamma' had always believed in. Her words became a source of strength, a reminder that I carried the potential to rise above any circumstance within me.

Family and friends' reactions were mixed. Some applauded my parents for their bold decision, while others thought they were insane.

A few even asked outright, "Are you doing this for money?"

My parents arranged a farewell party the day before we left for Chennai. It was a grand affair, another expense we could hardly afford. They invited family, Mummy's colleagues, Daddy's friends, and my classmates.

Our small home quickly became cramped with guests coming and going. Despite the heavy rain that day, no one left. The crowd felt overwhelming, and my grandparents, who had been staying with us for days, clung to the last moments we had together.

Some guests wished us well during the party, but others whispered behind our backs. No one knew what lay ahead for us.

I greeted everyone, accepted every piece of advice, and embraced each goodbye until the last guest left that evening.

By then, I was utterly exhausted, my head pounding with a migraine.

I had been diagnosed with migraines when I was ten. The pain was relentless—a throbbing, pulsating ache that made even the simplest moments unbearable. Each episode felt like a battle, something you could only endure and never truly escape. I saw doctor after doctor, hoping for a cure, a magic pill to stop it, but none existed. So, I learned to wait—suffer through the hours, sometimes days, until the pain decided to let me go.

That night, I slept with my parents.

My grandparents rested on the veranda, their presence a quiet comfort.

My headache was so intense that I could hardly rest my head on the pillow, the pain throbbing relentlessly through my skull.

Mummy, in her usual way, called for help from my grandmothers. They rushed in as if they were urgent care doctors, each bringing their own remedies.

One grandmother carried a small bowl of salt, the kind used to ward off the evil eye—Drishti, she called it. The other brought a broom, also meant to ward off ill fortune. They moved around me with ritualistic precision, muttering prayers, making sure to do everything they could to "make the pain vanish."

When they were done, they both felt sure my headache would disappear. They urged me to rest, and I tried, though the pain in my head was too much.

But at that moment, something shifted in my heart. I suddenly realized what I was about to leave behind. Who would be there to care for me in the U.S. when I had a migraine? Who would ward off the evil eye for me? Who would feed me with their hands, their love, their care? Who would shield me from painful moments? My heart was congested with pain; all these thoughts were rising in me.

Before we finally drifted to sleep, my parents placed their hands on me—firm, final.

"You must adjust, Ammulu," Mummy said, her voice steady but with something underneath it, something close to breaking.

"Help them as much as you can."

"Take care of your things."

"Study well."

"They must say, 'Padma raised her daughter well.'"

The words came one after another, their meaning heavy in the air, until they faltered.

The throbbing in my head matched the rhythm of their voices, and before I even realized it, I slipped into sleep, the weight of what was to come settling over me.

The biggest blessing for me as a child was sleep. In my early years, I struggled with nightmares—nightmares about snakes. They felt so real that sometimes they haunted me even after I woke up in the middle of the night. I'd see a snake slithering across Daddy, sleeping beside me. It was nerve-wracking, and those dreams still lingered in my mind. But eventually, the nightmares faded. No matter what happened during the day, I had sleep—a deep, peaceful sleep that allowed me to forget everything and find some semblance of calm.

I enjoyed this peace for only a few years, and shortly after my move to the U.S., that sense of calm I had found in sleep was also stolen from me.

When I woke up, the house was already in commotion. Both sets of grandmothers were on kitchen duty. Mummy was doing some final packing, trying to fill the suitcases with everything she could give me and more. Daddy greeted me with a kiss and handed me a glass of milk. I drank it with no urgency, no desire.

Mummy washed and braided my long hair one last time. For the farewell, I wore a bright orange dress.

I said goodbye to my grandparents, aunts, uncles, and friends, their faces blurred with unshed tears. My grandparents—who had seen the deaths of their children and the weight of loss too many times—couldn't contain their grief at parting with me.

They would never visit me. We all knew that. Would I ever return? What if I lost one of them when I was far away, and this was the last time I had them? The thought lodged itself in my chest like a thorn.

Even though it was the middle of the school day, my friends came to say goodbye. They carried small gifts—greeting cards and a jewelry box that, when opened, played music while a tiny ballet dancer twirled.

As a teenager, I believed my friends' love was more important than anything else—even more than my parents'. They understood me, or at least I thought they did, in ways my family never could. Their approval felt like everything.

Leaving them was also hard. I clutched the box to my chest, memorizing their faces, the warmth of their hugs. This was the last time we would stand together, laugh together, belong to the same world. As we drove away, I finally saw them in the rearview mirror. Their tears mirrored my own.

I wanted to cry openly, to let the grief spill out, but I wiped my face quickly. Mummy's discipline pressed down on me. Tears were a weakness I wasn't allowed to show.

The car moved forward, heavy with luggage, yet not nearly as heavy as the weight pressing against my chest.

With every twist and turn, every stretch of highway, I felt the pull of the inevitable.

I wanted time to stretch, for the journey to never end, but the road had no mercy.

The skyline of Chennai emerged, chaotic and unrelenting. Despite the storm raging within me, nothing could change what was coming.

We had arrived.

And there was no turning back.

In Chennai, I would leave my parents behind, board a plane for the first time, and step into the unknown.

The quietness of the car raised many questions in my mind.

Was it faith that gave them the strength to send me away? Stupidity? Desperation?

Would they have done this if I were a boy? *This question ate me away for many years to come.*

In the 1990s, in a middle-class family in southern India, a girl's birth was rarely met with celebration. Sons were desired, cherished, and seen as heirs, while daughters were burdens—expenses to be married off, responsibilities that never truly left. Some families went to the extreme, snuffing out a newborn girl's life before it even began. Others made their disappointment known in quieter, sharper ways—a sigh, a silence, a lingering sense of regret that never faded.

I always knew my parents never had a second child because their first—me—was a girl. And so, I wrestled with the question that never stopped haunting me. Did they give me away because I was a girl? Or did they send me away because, as a girl, they wanted me to have a life beyond the limits of our world?

I swung between both thoughts like a pendulum, unable to settle into one truth, trapped between abandonment and sacrifice.

I didn't ask these questions then. I hadn't yet learned to resent them.

At the time, I believed this was for my future. Daddy's business had failed, and they were making the ultimate sacrifice for me.

The resentment came later.

There was no room for emotion at my aunt's house in Chennai. The house overflowed with people—our families had gathered to see us off. It was crowded, chaotic, and loud.

Suitcases lined the walls, and people slept wherever they found space on the floor. My aunt and mother were confined to the kitchen, making meal after meal to feed the never-ending crowd.

In a few hours, we would leave for the airport. There were four of us actually traveling that day, but nearly twenty people came to see us off.

We piled into a massive truck, squeezing in alongside our twelve suitcases as if the sheer number of people could somehow lessen the weight of what was happening.

The airport felt like a different universe—one I had only seen in movies or imagined in distant dreams. Bright lights stretched endlessly, illuminating the vast space in a way that made the night outside feel even darker.

People moved with purpose, their suitcases rolling smoothly behind them, their eyes set on destinations I couldn't even guess.

The air hummed with an energy I had never felt before—voices speaking languages I didn't understand, faint robotic announcements echoing across the halls, and security scanners beeping.

Outside, sleek cars lined up, trunks popping open to swallow luggage as effortlessly as if they were made for it.

I stood frozen momentarily, gripping my bag, feeling impossibly small in the middle.

Back home, the loudest sound at night was the occasional barking of a stray dog or the distant call of a train passing through.

Here, the world never seemed to sleep.

I wasn't sure if I belonged in this place, in this rush, in this future that was now just a plane ride away.

But whether I was ready or not, there was no turning back.

We loaded our suitcases onto carts, too focused on the logistics of checking in to let the goodbyes sink in. Our families had to stay outside— only ticket holders were allowed past the entrance.

"We'll come back out after we check our bags," we reassured them. A half-truth. A way to soften the inevitable.

I gripped the trolley, pushing forward under the weight of my suitcases and something heavier—something unspoken.

We stood in line, carefully watching the person in front of us, hoping they knew the process better than we did.

When it was finally our time, we approached a counter that was open.

"Passports, please."

The agent at the counter said, barely looking up.

It was my first time traveling, but for him, we were just another set of passengers in a long line.

Our fumbling hands, our nervous glances—it was apparent we were just another set of passengers. We were first-timers.

I smiled, trying to appear friendly. Trying to be liked.

Even now, no matter how many times I travel—whether in business class or economy—that feeling lingers.

That quiet, unshakable sense of being less than.

Each suitcase that disappeared onto the conveyor belt carried more than just my belongings. It brought my parents' sacrifices, hard-earned money, and faith in a future they couldn't see.

We returned to our waiting family, but this time, a mesh screen separated us.

My parents stood on the other side, no longer able to touch me.

Silently, completely, they handed me over.

"Take care of her," they begged.

They treated me as if I were something fragile as if they were giving away something precious yet letting it go all the same.

Their hands trembled. Their voices cracked. Mummy wept harder.

And still, I turned away.

I had to be strong; I could not cry.

I didn't cry.

I said goodbye, looking into their eyes one last time.

This scene—holding back tears when leaving them—would repeat many times in the following years.

After many years, many visits, many goodbyes, not crying, I realized, wasn't healthy. Perhaps it was my way of protesting, of expressing the anger I couldn't voice. I told myself, "Why should I cry when they're willing to send me away?"

I wasn't sure why I thought that, but it created an invisible barrier around me. I thought it was an unhealthy pattern that I needed to break.

I finally did it, when I visited Mummy and Daddy after Covid shook the world. I cried, clutching Daddy like a child. A security guard, seeing me, thought I was traveling for the first time and tried to offer words of strength as he checked my passport.

We walked toward the gate.

A new life stretched ahead of me- a new family and country.

I told myself I should feel the excitement.

Instead, all I felt was a quiet, aching hollowness.

We carried our small suitcases and a blue folder with our paperwork. I held onto the tickets and passports, communicating when needed, until we finally reached our gate.

As we boarded the plane, a flight attendant greeted us with a bright smile.

"Welcome to Lufthansa Airlines."

"Thank you," I murmured, forcing my lips into a polite curve.

We found our seats in the middle row. I took the aisle seat, gripping the armrest as if it could anchor me.

The plane roared to life, shuddering as it lifted into the sky.

I stared out the window, watching my old life shrink beneath me.

The flight took off, and so did my strength.

The gates of my tears burst open, and for the next few minutes, I had no control over them.

I imagined my parents walking away from the airport, their shoulders slumped. Their hands empty, crying silently.

I imagined them returning to our home, quieter than it had ever been before.

Would they fall to the floor when they opened the doors and cry?

Would they stop living, eating, and sleeping in my memory?

A family of three, now reduced to two.

And me?

I was drifting further and further away, soaring into the unknown.

"Distance tests the depths of a bond."

Strange Beginnings

I was only fourteen when I boarded that flight—a child stepping into the unknown, carrying a fragile mix of determination and quiet fear.

I barely understood what lay ahead—every part of it felt unknown, overwhelming—but I told myself I would figure it out. Because if I didn't hold onto that hope if I let the fear take over, I might never be able to go. I had to believe I could manage it, even when a part of me wasn't sure.

It was my first time seeing a plane up close, let alone traveling on one. The same was true for my adoptive family. We were stepping into an unfamiliar world, one that felt as distant as the sky we were flying through. My heart felt heavy as I boarded, but there was no time to dwell on it. There were too many things to learn and small battles to fight just to make it to our destination.

The first in-flight meal was a shock.

The tray landed in front of me, filled with strange, foil-wrapped containers.

I had never used a knife and fork before. In India, we eat with our hands—how food tastes best. Eating with one's hands is more than just a tradition; it is an intimate, sensory experience that deepens the connection with food. Rooted in Ayurveda, it was believed that the fingertips activated digestive enzymes, preparing the body for nourishment. Beyond practicality, it symbolizes togetherness, fostering warmth and community during meals.

A spoon was the only utensil I occasionally used, and even that felt unnecessary most of the time. Now, I was expected to eat like the people around me, using a fork and a knife.

I peeled one container open, revealing a salad—something I had never eaten before in my life. I didn't know it was supposed to be paired with dressing. I picked at the cucumber and cherry tomatoes, confused by the uncooked green leaves that lay untouched on my plate.

Another container held rice and curry—or at least that's what it seemed to be. I took a bite, expecting warmth, spice, something familiar. Instead, the taste was bland and unappetizing. I swallowed a few bites but couldn't eat anymore.

This was my new reality. This was me taking baby steps towards adjusting to what was given to me and surviving.

I followed instructions meticulously, mimicking others when I wasn't sure what to do.

Customs, immigration, more security checks, more walking. My head spun with exhaustion, but I kept going, step after step, forcing myself to push through the haze of doubt.

Our layover was in Frankfurt, Germany. We followed a fellow passenger through the terminal for a while but soon realized that not everyone from our flight would be boarding the one to Dallas. I had to figure out how to read the screens with gate assignments, follow the signs through the airport, and navigate to the right gate while lugging our overpacked carry-ons. By the time we boarded, it felt like we had swum across an ocean. And then—after what felt like an eternity—we landed in Dallas, Texas.

It was a whirlwind of firsts. A crash course in independence. It began a journey that would shape me in ways I couldn't yet imagine. And the first time, I was far away from Mummy's watchful eyes.

When we stepped out of the airport, dragging our luggage behind us, it felt like we were the last to leave. The terminal was nearly empty, the earlier rush replaced by an eerie quiet.

Our sponsoring mom was there, waiting. She stood stiffly beside the car, arms crossed, her handbag clutched too tightly under her arm. When we approached, she offered a polite nod—not a smile, not a hug, just a nod.

We all greeted her cordially, unsure of what to expect. Her red lipstick was applied with precision, but her expression remained unreadable. She shifted her weight from one foot to the other, anxious to get going or uncomfortable being watched. Her eyes never lingered on any of us too long.

It felt new. Forced. Like we were all actors playing roles in a scene, none of us had rehearsed. Everyone was on their best behavior, polite but distant, careful but uncertain. No one knew who the others were beneath the surface. We were strangers carrying the weight of obligation, stitched together by paperwork and promises—but not by love.

I admired the sponsoring mom. Even though Mummy worked, which was uncommon for the women in my family, the sponsoring mom was different. She drove to the airport, had a job, wore make-up, and spoke English with an accent—it all felt foreign yet fascinating.

I sat in the back of the car, pressing my face against the window, utterly mesmerized by the sight of Dallas unfolding before me.

The flyovers—layers upon layers of roads stacked high in the sky— left me speechless. I had lived my whole life in a small South Indian village, where the streets were narrow, familiar, and often shared with cows and stray dogs. I had only ever visited a big city a handful of times, and even then, nothing came close to this. These highways in Dallas looked like they belonged to another world entirely. I couldn't believe cars actually drove on them—so high above the ground, curving and crisscrossing like ribbons in the sky. They felt magical, impossible, like something out of a science fiction movie. I pressed my face to the window, trying to take it all in, wide-eyed and disoriented. This wasn't just a new country—it was another planet.

The weather didn't strike me as notably different, but everything else felt like a dream.

We arrived at our new home—on the outside, it looked big and was a one-story. As we arrived, the garage door rumbled to life, groaning like a giant awakening from sleep. As it slowly lifted, revealing the world beyond, I stood frozen, my eyes wide with wonder. Back home, doors were pushed, pulled, or latched with rusted bolts—but this? This was something else. It moved independently, like an invisible hand was lifting it with effortless grace. To me, it felt like watching the mouth of a cave open by itself, an entrance to something unknown, something powerful. I had never seen a door obey without touch, and the sponsoring mom parked the car directly inside the house.

We exited the car and stepped inside the home through the garage door, our suitcases rolling to a stop in the living room. The sponsoring dad was waiting for us at home, anticipating our arrival. His greeting was brief, lacking warmth. There was no hugging between the brothers or a moment of affection.

He looked exhausted, worn down in a way beyond mere tiredness. His hair was completely gray, and his movements were slow, almost weighed down. He seemed older than my grandfather, despite my grandfather having fifteen years on him.

We all sat in an awkward silence, broken only by a few polite questions about our journey and our short, hesitant answers. The air felt heavy and unfamiliar.

After a few minutes, we were shown to a room. Grateful for the privacy, we freshened up, washing away the fatigue of travel, and then retreated for the night, letting exhaustion pull us into sleep.

The first few days were a whirlwind as we absorbed everything.

I was taking in the sights, sounds, and unspoken rules of this new country. The way the microwave could heat food in seconds felt like magic. The oversized fridge, stocked with more food than I had ever seen in one place, was a luxury I had never known existed. Hot and cold water flowed effortlessly from the faucets without needing to boil or fetch it by hand. With their steady streams of water, the showers replaced the bucket and mug I had always known. Every detail, from the carpeted floors to the humming air conditioner, was a quiet reminder of how different this world was from the one I had left behind.

Adrenaline, jet lag, endless paperwork—Social Security cards, school enrollments, medical check-ups—it all happened too fast, a whirlwind of bureaucracy that left no room for emotions or space to process the enormity of what was unfolding.

We were enrolled in a school farther from the sponsor's home because it offered an ESL program. Before classes began, I was tested for my spoken English skills—and to my surprise, I did well.

Back home in our small South Indian village, English had never been my first language, but it had never been something I struggled with either. My English teacher, George Sir, had seen to that. He drilled pronunciation into us, challenged us beyond grammar exercises, and taught us how to think and express ourselves in English—not just follow rules. His lessons have stayed with me.

Some teachers leave a mark. George Sir was one of them. He's part of the reason I write today.

Despite my test results, I opted to join the ESL program when given the choice.

Not because I couldn't handle regular classes. I could. But my confidence wavered in this new world, where everything felt foreign— from how people dressed to how they laughed. I wasn't ready to stand out, to be the girl with the funny accent in a room full of native speakers.

The sponsoring dad's sister and her children, whom I will refer to throughout the book as "The Other Family" had arrived months before us, also living under the same roof. She had a son in his late twenties and a daughter in her early twenties. I felt closer to them than to my adoptive family or the sponsor family. I had met the daughter years ago at a family event in India, and her presence was a small comfort in this unfamiliar place.

Right before we arrived, both she and her brother found jobs at a grocery store. They spent their evenings and days off with us, filling the emptiness and easing the loneliness, if only for a while.

The house that has four bedrooms and two bathrooms was spacious. Coming from a home of only three people and tiny rooms, this felt very different.

The master bedroom, the room farthest away from the main door, had an attached bathroom and was connected to a long living room, while the three other bedrooms shared a single bathroom. The house was large, but with so many people crammed inside, space felt tight.

The sponsor's daughter had her room and used the master bathroom with her parents. Their son stayed in the master bedroom with his mother. The sponsoring father sat, slept, ate, and did almost everything, claiming his spot on the living room sofa, parked in front of the TV, where he had the best view of the screen and the kitchen.

Our adopted family of four squeezed into one bedroom. The Other Family of three took another.

Each night, I lay awake, staring at the unfamiliar ceiling, my mind churning with thoughts I couldn't quiet. This wasn't home. It didn't feel like it ever could be. I had left everything behind for this. There was no turning back. So I wanted to love it.

From the very beginning, something fell off in that house. The sponsoring dad rarely moved from his spot in front of the television, except to use the bathroom. Some days, he was sullen and withdrawn, with a dark and impenetrable mood. On other days, he was oddly cheerful, cracking jokes like he had woken up to a different life. He didn't work; his income came from a disability check.

On the other hand, the sponsoring mom carried the full weight of the household. She worked twelve-hour shifts four days a week, with exhaustion clinging to her like a second skin.

Their love for their children was evident, but the balance in their lives was skewed. He stayed home, watching TV day and night, while she worked herself to the bone. Their dynamic was fragile, teetering on the edge of unspoken resentment. We, the newcomers, were soon part of that dynamic.

On the first day of school, we woke up before sunrise and got ready with excitement and my loose-fitting clothes.

Our adoptive mom, trying to offer us some comfort, quietly set out leftover rice and rasam—a warm, tangy soup that smelled like home. She had learned how to warm food in the microwave and set it in front of us. The steam curled into the air like a fragile invitation.

I hadn't eaten since the previous afternoon, and the scent made my stomach ache harder.

I sat down, fingers reaching for the plate, when the sponsoring dad's voice sliced through the quiet. "We only provide one meal daily in this house," he said. "They have to get used to eating at school. There's free lunch." His tone was flat and final, like a rule being recited, not a decision being questioned. The moment froze.

Our adoptive mom paused. She didn't speak. She didn't defend us. She looked away and cleared the table. I stared at the plate that was no longer mine.

The rasam's scent hung in the air—warm tamarind, mustard seeds, home. It smelled of care, of mornings when Ammamma would gently blow on my spoon and say, "Eat this; it'll make you strong." I reached for it—and was pulled back. The plate was gone. So was home.

A rush of sadness surged inside me, rising so fast it threatened to drown me. I wanted to cry. Not just for the food but for the comfort it represented—the kind I had left behind. But I couldn't. I didn't have the luxury of tears or the time to fall apart. There was no room in this new life for softness, needs, or breakdowns. So I swallowed it all—the hunger, the hurt, the longing—and washed my plate in silence.

Our adoptive mom hesitated but didn't argue. It wasn't her house. These weren't her rules. We weren't her children. She didn't fight for us.

I thought of Mummy. She would have insisted. She would have fought. She would never let me go to school hungry. A lump formed in my throat, but I swallowed it down. Quietly, I put my plate away, washing it under cold water.

I left the house with an ache in my stomach, not just from hunger but from something more profound. The first wave of homesickness hit me then, sharp and unrelenting.

"Forget the past, but remember the lesson."

The Breaking

I walked out of the house, the empty ache in my belly mirroring the hollow feeling inside me. We waited outside for the school bus, feeling the chilly air. A yellow school bus stopped in front of us, and the automatic doors opened. I noticed our driver was an Indian man, who I later found out also taught at the school. That dual role confused me.

In India, professions were divided. Drivers drove. Teachers taught. The overlap suggested hardship, but it also offered a small comfort—a familiar face in unfamiliar territory. Though he never taught me directly, he'd often smile and wave when he saw me in school.

As the year went on, I cried silently on the bus more often than I'd like to admit. My face turned to the window, hiding the tears I couldn't explain. If he noticed, he never mentioned it. Sometimes, he asked how I was adjusting, but we never connected beyond those polite exchanges. Still, his presence was a thread that tied me to home, however faintly.

My first class was Physical Education. Back in India, sports and physical education were more of an afterthought, especially in high school, where science and math took precedence over everything, so I wasn't sure what to expect. As I stepped into the gym, I was overwhelmed by its sheer size—it felt massive, with at least twenty rows of bleachers on either side, towering basketball hoops at both ends and a floor that stretched wider than the outdoor playground at my old school.

When the teacher announced a free period, the space burst into life— balls bounced, sneakers squeaked, kids shouted and laughed. I stood at the edge, unsure what to do, before finally picking up a badminton racket.

I swung clumsily, missing every shot, but it was something—something that made me feel a little less invisible.

Then I saw something that stopped me cold.

A couple sat on the bleachers, kissing and cuddling—right in front of the teacher. I froze. In my world, that would've been scandalous and severely punishable. But here, no one reacted. The teacher didn't seem to like it, but she chose to pick her battles and focused her attention on the rest of my classmates.

I spent the first day—and then the first week—learning the school's layout, figuring out where each class was, the quickest paths to get from one to the next without being late, how to find my way to the cafeteria for the free breakfast and lunch, and making sure I caught the right bus home at the end of the day.

At school, I barely touched the food. The cold milk, the unfamiliar tastes, and smells were nauseating—it was all too much to stomach.

I waited until the evening for the one meal we were given.

Despite the initial confusion, I fell in love with school. Not just because it was different from the rigid, fear-driven system I knew but because it was kind. Teachers treated us like equals. There were no uniforms, no forced conformity. Kids wore miniskirts, dyed their hair blue or pink, and moved through the hall with confidence, I had never seen before.

Even though I was placed in ninth grade—despite finishing eleventh in India—I didn't mind. The academics were easy. I breezed through math, science, and English. I struggled a bit with American geography but was eager to learn. What mattered most wasn't the content; I felt safe and belonged in those classrooms.

I didn't make many friends. Cordial, polite conversations came and went, but I was too guarded to form real bonds. We'd been warned, "Be careful who you talk to," and I obeyed. My sponsoring parents believed that the world was plotting against us and that we must guard ourselves.

But there was one person who broke through my shell—Mrs. Fields, my ESL teacher. A small woman with a gentle voice, she offered me more than grammar lessons. Her classroom was a sanctuary. If I had free time, I would go to her. She kept snacks, gave me books, taught me to use a computer, and encouraged me to write.

She's another big reason I'm able to write this now.

Some days, I fantasized about her adopting me, about living in a home with her where I was safe, cared for, and seen. But God had other plans.

That house I returned to each day after a blissful time in school was worlds apart. It was a kingdom of madness—loud, chaotic, and cruel. Shouting matches erupted over anything and everything: money, food, even someone pausing too long at a window. The sponsoring parents lived in a constant state of paranoia, convinced everyone around them was out to get them. That fear clung to the walls and seeped into every interaction, poisoning the air we breathed.

It wasn't just the noise that wore me down but the constant manipulation. Gossip was the currency there. Adults used us like pawns, whispering lies and half-truths into our ears and asking us to report on one another— friendships dissolved under the weight of suspicion. We were kids thrown into a game we never asked to play, drained of joy and trust.

I dreaded weekends because they meant staying home, which exposed me to everything that made that place unbearable: the shouting, the silence, and the careful tiptoeing around moods that turned without warning. But the most challenging part came every Sunday.

That's when my parents called from India, using an internet phone at a local café. "Sushmitha, phone call for you," the sponsoring dad would announce. I'd take the cordless phone to the hallway and try to carve out a moment of privacy, always aware that someone could be listening from the other room.

Mummy always spoke first, her voice warm and cheerful. Daddy's turn would undo me; the sound of him saying "Hello" shattered my composure. I cried every time, not because of anything he said—but because I couldn't say anything. I couldn't tell them the truth—that I was scared, hungry, and lonely. They thought I was just homesick and told me to be strong.

And so, I was. Or at least I pretended to be.

But strength in that house meant survival.

I carved out a sliver of peace in that noise and chaos—a small, dark closet. I'd curl up inside it with Shiva's Fire, the first book I ever borrowed from the school library. It told the story of Parvati, a gifted girl born during a fierce storm in southern India. She, too, carried something powerful and strange inside her—something that set her apart. As she made her way to a dance school in Madras and confronted the weight of destiny, I saw myself in her. Through her story, I found something I hadn't felt anywhere else in that house: safety. That was when my love of reading took root—because books, unlike people, didn't hurt me; they held me.

Still, I couldn't read my way out of the hunger.

I had known anger. I had heard screaming.

But I had never known the ache of real hunger.

Back home, even in scarcity, food was sacred. No one was ever turned away. Here, food became a tool of control.

One night, the sponsoring mom made ground turkey with spices. The aroma filled the house like a promise. I watched as she fed her children rice balls with her own hands. The rest of us got watery rasam and potato chips—again.

I didn't ask for more. I didn't cry—not where anyone could see. But that night, the rasam tasted even blander than usual. Maybe it was the salt of my silent tears that gave it any flavor at all. I didn't know back then to expect to be treated equally as their children, even if it only meant a plateful of rice and curry, wasn't acceptable. We were under their charity and a burden, and instead of being grateful for what was given, I was being greedy. To hope for something that was never meant to nourish me.

Even now, the smell of ground turkey drags me back—to that room, that hunger, that feeling of being othered and forgotten.

Recently, I met a 19-year-old girl my nonprofit had supported since she was nine. She shared a painful experience from her stay with an extended family while taking her final exams that year—her own home was in turmoil, leaving her no choice but to live with them.

She told me they refused to feed her or send her to school with a packed lunch. They made her sit outside until bedtime and, if she was on her period, treated her as untouchable.

Her words struck a deep chord in me as she recounted these hardships. The memories of my suffering in this house came rushing back—I knew that pain all too well. Without a word, I pulled her into an embrace, tears streaming down my face.

Food, love, and peace were painfully scarce in that house. What had started as a hopeful chapter in a foreign land quickly became a daily struggle for survival—a battle against hunger, neglect, and the suffocating weight of fear.

In fifth grade, I got into an argument with a classmate. Words flew between us—sharp, fast, and escalating—until she dared me to hit her. And I did. Without hesitation, I slapped her.

At the time, it didn't feel wrong. I felt a little proud of myself, too.

That's how I'd seen conflict handled growing up. Physical punishment wasn't just common—it was expected. Teachers used it to enforce obedience, and parents wielded it like a right. We weren't taught that "hands are not for hitting." We were shown that adults had the power to hit, and children had to endure without resistance.

When Mummy disciplined me, I accepted it—not because it didn't hurt, but because it was normalized. Pain was supposed to teach, and fear was supposed to earn respect. So, when I hit my classmate, it wasn't defiance; it was a learned behavior.

It wasn't until I came to the U.S. that the world shifted around me—and inside me. I saw adults lose their tempers like those back home, but their anger terrified me this time.

I knew now that it wasn't normal. I noticed how my body braced itself, even when no one raised a hand. I began to understand that the lessons I had carried with me weren't universal truths—they were cycles of harm.

That slap stayed with me, not because I was proud, but because I didn't even know it was wrong.

It took years of unlearning to realize that discipline shouldn't be born of fear and that respect should never be demanded through pain.

I had to teach myself that love doesn't come with bruises and that hands should never be used for hurting—not by anyone, not for any reason.

I can endure major surgery and refuse pain medication afterward—by choice. I've weathered migraines that score a 10/10 on the pain scale. Yet, when my son playfully slaps my back in passing, a jolt of agony shoots through me.

Logically, I know it's just my mind—my body misreading a harmless, joyful gesture as a threat, shaped by the past. But no amount of reasoning stops the instinctive flinch, the visceral reaction I wish I could control.

That experience of hunger and fear in that house has changed the way I live. Today, no one leaves my home hungry—not physically, not emotionally.

I protect peace fiercely. I speak gently, even when angry, because I remember living in a house where your entire body clenches at the sound of keys in the door. I lead my team with empathy and gentleness at work and never encourage disrespect. That's how I choose to break the cycle.

"A few bad chapters don't define your whole story."

The Night's Betrayal

Living under hostile conditions forces people to shrink—to become invisible, as if willing themselves into nonexistence. They move silently, careful not to draw attention. That was life in that house, in the rooms we were given.

Lights stayed off. Voices stayed low. Laughter was rare; smiles, even rarer. No one asked about each other's day—not the adults, not the kids, not in our adoptive family, nor The Other Family who lived there.

In those few months, another unthinkable horror unfolded in that darkness—a darkness that crept into the only peace I had left: sleep.

Sleep had been my only escape, a fragile pocket of quiet where hunger and fear couldn't reach me. In those stolen hours, I could pretend I was home again—safe, loved, whole. But even that small comfort was taken from me.

In the stillness of the night, I felt a presence beside me—close, too close. A hand brushed against my skin, and breath touched my neck. It started with fleeting touches, soft enough to be dismissed as a dream. I wanted so badly to believe it was a dream.

For a few fleeting moments, I told myself it was a memory—my grandmother stroking my hair as she sang me to sleep, her stories of Lord Rama and Krishna washing over me like a lullaby. She would kiss my forehead and whisper, "Minnamma," full of love.

But this was not my grandmother. This was not love. This was something darker—calculated, predatory.

I didn't know how to name it then. I only knew it felt wrong.

The act never escalated fully, not physically—there were always too many people in the room, and that fact that suffocated me the most protected me. But that didn't make it any less horrifying.

Once he understood that I was obliged to his attempts, he tried to lure me away under the pretense of privacy: "Let's go sit in the car and talk to your parents in private," he'd say. And I went. Because I was desperate—for a call home, food, and the illusion of being seen. That desperation was twisted into a weapon against me.

He used my longing for care as bait. Sometimes it was food. Sometimes it was a kind word. Sometimes it was the offer of freedom, just for a moment, from the suffocating cruelty of the house.

And I let myself believe it. I needed to accept it. Because in a house with no love, even sick attention felt like affection. And that is one of the most painful truths I carry.

I convinced myself it was a transactional system—the price I had to pay. If I stayed quiet and complied with his demands, I'd feel the attention, even if only for a moment. So I let him take his sick pleasure from invading my space, even as my skin crawled with the need to tear off every place he touched.

But silence isn't just survival; it's fuel for an abuser. It emboldens them and feeds their cruelty day by day. They thrive on the power of your fear, your submission—a twisted sustenance drawn from your suffering.

Dr. Gabor Maté, in The Myth of Normal, writes that abusers are adept at sensing which children are least likely to speak out. That was me. My silence was predictable, and he knew it. He calculated it. That's how predators work—they don't just find victims by accident. They look for the quiet ones. The ones who already know how to disappear.

I didn't fight back. I didn't scream. I just lay there, night after night, pretending to sleep. Frozen. Terrified. My body braced at the sound of footsteps, my heart pounding with dread. I told myself it wasn't real. That if I kept my eyes closed, it wouldn't be happening. That it was better than the screaming, the hunger, the humiliation.

Because growing up in India, this wasn't new. Predators had many faces: teachers, neighbors, uncles. No one talked about it. There were no rules, no conversations, no safe places. I had no words for it, no concept that what was happening to me was wrong. I was a child who thought she had invited it—by smiling, speaking, and existing.

I carried that belief with me across the ocean. And in that house, it took root all over again.

So, I stayed silent. And my silence let it continue.

Not speaking didn't mean I didn't feel. I felt everything: shame, confusion, and self-loathing. I began to hate him. I hated that house. I hated Mummy and Daddy for sending me there. I hated God. But mostly, I hated myself—for not running, for not screaming, for not being stronger.

I thought it was my fault.

It took me years—years of therapy, of journaling, of sitting with the wounded child inside me—to finally understand the truth: none of it was my fault. I was fourteen. A child. A child longing for safety, love, and someone to notice that I was hurting. And no child, under any circumstance, asks to be violated. No smile, no hunger, no desperate need for comfort can ever be mistaken for consent.

But in that house, I didn't know that on those nights.

And so, I endured.

As the abuse escalated, he may have convinced himself I liked it and that I was complicit in his sickness. But I wasn't even old enough to understand what was happening, let alone give consent. I wasn't silent because I wanted it—I was silent because I didn't know I had the right to say no. Because I had never seen a world where this was called abuse. Only one where they were expected to survive in silence or avoid it by being invisible.

If you are responsible for a child – if you have the opportunity to guide, protect, or care for them – let this be something you never leave unsaid. "Abuse is not your fault."

Speak to them often and loudly about their worth, safety, and right to boundaries. Teach them, not with whispers but with unwavering certainty, that their bodies belong to them and no one has the right to violate that.

Because in the tragic event that abuse happens, their mind will try to deceive them. It may tell them they were asking for it. That they were acting like a slut. That it doesn't happen to "good kids." But if you have already armed them with the truth, they will not fall for these lies. They will not mistake abuse for shame.

Instead, they will know—without hesitation—that what happened was wrong. That no one, no matter their authority or relation, has the right to touch them in a way that makes them feel unsafe.

Most importantly, they will know that silence is not their only option. That safety is something they can seek and deserve to pursue. And that the bravest, most powerful thing they can do is gather every ounce of courage and get to it.

This is the gift you can give them—not just love or protection, but the knowledge that no matter what happens, they are never to blame and never have to endure it alone.

To the Fourteen-Year-Old Me (and Every Kid Who Needs to Hear This)

I know you wonder if it was really abuse because you didn't fight it—because you liked the attention. After all, it made you feel special, because, for a moment, it felt like love. But hear me when I say this: It was abuse. It was never your fault.

They were older. They knew better. They should have protected you, not taken advantage of your loneliness, need for love, and longing to feel safe. The way you were treated at home, the way no one was there to protect you—that does not make what they did okay. You told yourself it didn't matter as long as you didn't think about what was happening to your body, but that was survival, not consent.

You were a child. You should have been safe.

I need you to know this: Your worth is not defined by what someone else did to you. You are not broken. You are not to blame. You have the right to be angry. You have the right to grieve. And most of all, you have the right to heal.

One day, you'll look back and see how strong you were. But for now, hold on. Hold on to the parts of you that are still soft, still hopeful. The world hasn't taken everything from you. And no matter what, you are still whole. You are still you. And that is enough.

"A good future will have some bad memories."

Uncelebrated

The Other Family was preparing to leave. Their departure felt inevitable after the fights in the house escalated from shouting matches to physical altercations. I had imagined their leaving would bring some relief, a semblance of peace to the turmoil that had become our daily existence.

Just before they left, my birthday arrived.

It was my first birthday in the U.S., and I had just turned fifteen. I woke up with a fragile kind of hope fluttering in my chest. Maybe today would be different. Maybe there would be no fights, shouting, or hunger—just one peaceful day. I slipped into one of the Indian dresses Mummy had lovingly packed for me—a vibrant piece of home I could carry on my skin.

That morning, my parents called from the unreliable internet cafe. The line cutting in and out, "Happy Birthday, Ammulu," Mummy said, her voice warm through the crackling line. I smiled, letting her words wrap around me like a desperately needed hug. I spoke to them with energy I hadn't felt in weeks. Then Daddy also wished me and I responded with all smiles. It was my birthday, after all. If there was ever a day to feel seen and loved—this was it.

My birthday fell on Thanksgiving that year. Everyone was home—the sponsoring mom, my cousins from The Other Family, the kids. The women in the house were cooking a feast: chicken curry (my favorite), ground turkey fry with sautéed onions, vegetable pulao, basmati rice cooked with spices, coconut milk, and vegetables, and raita, a cooling yogurt dish mixed with onions and cucumbers.

The aroma filled the air, rich and warm, stirring something inside me. For a moment, I let myself believe that the house might feel normal, even human, for once.

Then, I saw the cake.

It was sitting on the coffee table, waiting for me—a cake with blue and white cream on top, something I had never seen before.

Back home, my birthday cakes were either homemade or from the local bakery, looking more like sweet bread than an actual cake. This one felt special, almost magical.

Maybe, just maybe, this day would be different.

The dining table was filled with drinks, fruits, and cookies—an array of dishes that made my mouth water. In India, my birthday didn't fall on a holiday, and I had always celebrated it with friends at school. But here, it coincided with Thanksgiving—a holiday that, I would later learn, only added to my miseries.

I approached the cake table, hesitating for a moment before picking up the knife. The soft hum of chatter faded around me.

Then, the room erupted into song.

"Happy birthday to you, happy birthday to you, happy birthday to Sushmitha!" Sushmitha is my formal name that doesn't come with love and warmth of home, instead of Minnu. But I decided today is not the day to notice these things and feel low.

The voices blended, warm and cheerful. A wide smile spread across my face as I leaned forward to blow out the candles. For those few fleeting moments, the weight of my pain lifted, replaced by something rare—joy.

I fed the cake to my cousins first, then to my new parents, followed by the sponsoring parents. It was a small act of gratitude, a way to share the happiness I so desperately wanted to hold onto.

"Open the presents, Sushmitha," the sponsoring mom said, her voice carrying a rare note of thoughtfulness.

I received a handful of presents, each wrapped in colorful paper. I opened them carefully, making sure I didn't tear the wrapping. Back home, birthdays were simpler—my grandparents would give me money (which most mothers would confiscate anyway), my parents would buy a new outfit, and I'd distribute candies at school. That was it.

But here, for the first time, I was receiving gifts.

Among all the gifts I received that day, one stood out—a Walkman with big, over-the-head headphones. There were no cassettes to play, no music waiting to soothe me. But that didn't matter. It wasn't about the sound. It was about the promise. The idea that someday, I could slip away into a world of melody, into a quiet that belonged only to me.

I held it like it was sacred, a small portal to peace in a world that offered me none. In the following months, that silent Walkman became more than just a device—it became my companion, my armor. And when I finally had tapes to play, music poured into my ears like medicine.

But at that moment, my greatest gift was the food.

I had never felt so grateful for food before. Back home, my parents ensured I was always well-fed and satisfied. My lunch box was full of things I loved, and I never hesitated to share it with classmates. I remember asking Mummy, with the innocence only a child can have, "What does hunger feel like? Is it that empty ache in the tummy?" I asked because I truly didn't know.

But in that house, everything changed. Food was no longer a source of comfort—it became a source of fear, of control. It was rationed, withheld, used to remind us of our place. Hunger wasn't just physical; it was emotional, too. It gnawed at my body and my spirit.

And so, when someone offered me something to eat—anything, even a plate of rice—I received it like a treasure. I had never known how deeply grateful one could feel for food until I knew what it was to be denied it. That day, more than anything else, food felt like love.

Everyone was laughing, enjoying themselves, celebrating my birthday. The atmosphere was light and cheerful, filled with chatter and laughter. Then, suddenly, something shifted. I'm not sure what happened, but the energy in the room changed, and it grew uncomfortably quiet.

Instead of heading to the table as planned, The Other Family retreated to their room. The sponsoring parents disappeared into the master bedroom. My adoptive family and I returned to ours. The table stayed full and untouched.

No one ate. No one cared whether I did.

It was my birthday, and I was left to starve again while a table was covered with untouched food.

After waiting a few hours, hoping that things would change, I took off my dress, climbed into bed, and cried frustrated, defeated but silent tears.

That day, I made a silent vow to myself. I would never let my birthday pass unnoticed again. No matter where I was or what I had, I would celebrate it—and not just for myself. I would celebrate others, too. I would bake the cake, hang the lights, write the cards, and make people feel seen.

Because birthdays, I realized, are sacred. They're not just about getting older—they're about being acknowledged being remembered, especially for those who have felt invisible the rest of the year.

It takes so little to make someone feel special. And it's so cruel not to try—especially on the one day that belongs entirely to them.

That night, the house erupted. *The reason I do not know to this day.*

On this particular day, the altercation went beyond words. Adults chased each other with baseball bats. Curse words flew like weapons. The sponsoring dad, already simmering with anger and what I assumed were untreated psychological issues, became even more volatile. My adoptive father sided with The Other Family that was leaving, making things worse.

Every minute in that house felt like torture.

I often felt sad for the sponsoring parents' kids, too. What kind of life were they living? My parents had sent me to a family that was deeply troubled, abusive, cruel, and unhappy. At least I had a few years of normalcy when I lived with Mummy and Daddy. But for the sponsor kids, they had turned their home into hell, raised the kids in it and brought others (us) into it to suffer alongside them.

When The Other Family finally left to rent their apartment, they found freedom.

Though we endured the same harsh conditions, I always believed they had it better—because they had their mother. She shielded them. She fought to feed them, to pack their lunches even when the sponsoring father refused. On the hardest days, they had love binding them together—a trio who dried each other's tears and gathered strength for the battles ahead.

We shared the same house, but not the same war.

But their departure left behind an even angrier, more bitter sponsoring dad. We bore the brunt of his rage, and the sponsoring mom joined in.

Slowly and surely, the hunger left me. The desire to eat had died.

Mummy and Daddy still knew nothing.

Every week, when they called to check on me, I cried. I still cried. Everything I was holding on to that entire week would flow freely in tears. Not loudly, not messily—just quiet sobs that slipped out before I could stop them. They thought I was homesick.

"It's been months," they'd say gently. "Why are you still crying?"

They still had no idea that I was living in a nightmare.

I couldn't tell them the truth—not just because fear sat like a stone in my chest, but because the sponsoring parents had a habit of eavesdropping from another line. I never knew who was on the other end, silently gathering every word. So I swallowed the truth, over and over, until it rotted inside me.

I clenched my jaw until it hurt and ground my teeth until they ached. I wanted to scream, to beg for someone to come to get me—but all that ever came out was a thin, strangled cry. A sound so small it barely escaped past my lips.

It felt like my voice had been stolen, tucked away behind everything I couldn't say. The communication skills my mother nurtured for years that helped me obtain the visa to this hell were forgotten.

Later, I learned that when other families—people my parents knew in the U.S.— called to check in or speak to me, they were told I wasn't home.

I was "asleep," or "out," or "not feeling well."

But the truth was more straightforward than that.

The sponsors were afraid.

Afraid I might open my mouth.

Afraid I might finally say what was happening behind their doors.

Afraid that someone—anyone—might listen.

Might believe me.

It might save me.

"Forget the past, but remember the lesson."

Echoes of Resilience

A few years before I moved to the U.S., I attended a family function—a gathering filled with laughter, music, and the clinking of plates. Relatives I hadn't seen in years were there, their voices mingling in the air, thick with the scent of spices and the warmth of shared stories. It should have been a happy memory. But one moment from that night burned itself into my mind, never to be forgotten.

In the middle of the celebration, a relative turned to me, their smirk sharp and cruel. Their voice carried just far enough for others to hear, laced with cruelty.

"So, is your mother still hitting you? Are you still scared of her?"

The words landed like a slap. The chatter around us seemed to stop. My face burned with humiliation, my pulse roaring in my ears. I imagined every pair of eyes turning toward me, waiting, watching. Judging.

I swallowed hard, forcing an uncomfortable smile, my lips trembling. I wanted to say something—anything—but the words lodged in my throat. A tightness coiled in my chest, and a familiar feeling of shame crept in.

Why would they say that? Did they think it was funny? Did they even care what those words did to me?

I wish adults understood how deeply their words could wound a child. They throw out careless remarks, never realizing that those words echo in our minds for years, shaping our sense of self-worth—or destroying it.

Yes, Mummy had a temper. Yes, there were moments when I feared her anger. But she was complicated, flawed, human. And in that moment, standing under the weight of their stares, I hated the way that single question had reduced my entire childhood to something ugly and pitiful.

I thought leaving for the U.S. would be my ticket to freedom. I thought I was leaving behind fear.

I didn't know then that the world had much worse to offer than a strict mother.

My growing interest in school led me to excel—straight A's, awards, and praise from teachers for my discipline and character. It was one of the few areas where I felt a sense of achievement, a place where I could stand out in a valued way. But the contrast was painfully sharp.

At school, I was seen as a good student with promise. Yet, at home, I felt anything but that. There, I felt unwanted, invisible, like a shadow passing through a world that didn't care to see me. The accolades and recognition from school couldn't fill the emptiness I felt inside. I was praised for the person I was becoming at school, but the person I was at home felt lost in a suffocating silence.

I wasn't old enough to get a job—not yet fifteen—so I found my way to earn. I walked through the neighborhood, knocking on doors and offering to clean homes. Some people said yes. Others hesitated, wary of trusting their big houses to a teenage girl.

When they did say yes, I scrubbed and vacuumed with everything I had. Hours of labor for twenty dollars—my first real earnings, my first taste of independence.

Soon, my adoptive family caught on. They began joining in—splitting the work and dividing the profits. Twenty dollars meant equal shares; forty meant fleeting grins.

But we were never parent and child. Money changed hands like a transaction between partners. A real mother would've taken it all, insisting she was saving it for me. I might've resented it—but that's what parents do. That's how they protect.

My adoptive parents, they never wanted to be parents. Just parties to an arrangement. But that happiness didn't last.

The sponsoring parents found out. They found out when we came home and were excited to share the news of earnings with them.

A fight erupted—loud, vicious, final. They put an end to it. We weren't allowed to do this.

The sponsoring parents didn't explain why. There were only ultimatums, raised voices, and sudden bursts of anger right after they found out. But it felt like the real reason was fear.

Earning meant independence. Independence meant power. And power meant we could leave—just like The Other Family had. Maybe there were rules they were afraid of, things we didn't understand. But they never said that. All we saw was control, and all we felt was captivity. So we were back to sulking inside the home, walking on landmines ready to erupt.

Even in the darkest stretches, there were rare flickers of relief. Mrs. Fields, my ESL teacher, would sometimes ask permission—though it was always the sponsoring parents who truly had the final say—to take me and my adoptive sibling to her home for a meal.

The first time we stepped into her house, it was like crossing another world. The air smelled of something sweet and homemade. The guest room she showed us had a gentle Southern charm—soft lighting, a well-made bed, and a quilt draped with delicate flowers. There was a bathroom just for us to use. It was nothing grand, but it felt like dignity—like grace.

I sat quietly in her kitchen that evening, watching her husband slice a watermelon with slow, thoughtful precision. The room buzzed with small talk and soft laughter, and a breeze drifted through the open window. It was all so peaceful, so ordinary—and that's what made it feel extraordinary.

Because it reminded us of what we didn't have.

In that moment, surrounded by warmth and kindness, I felt something loosen in my chest. It wasn't joy. It was grief—the kind of grief that sneaks in when you remember what it feels like to be treated gently and how long it's been since you were.

My kind English teacher—her touch was like sunlight breaking through storm clouds. When she spoke, her hand would brush my arm, gentle as a falling leaf. She hugged me to say hello, her warmth lingering long after she pulled away. Sometimes, when I sat at her computer to check my email, she would stand behind me and rest her hands lightly on my shoulders, guiding me through each click and command. Her fingers never gripped, never demanded—only steadied.

To others, this might just be a cultural difference—Americans show love with physical gestures, while Indians are reserved and loved from a distance. But in that house, where touch was either absent or violent, her hands were lifelines. Every brush of her fingers, every casual embrace, sent tiny currents of electricity through me, jolting my heart back to life. She didn't know it, but those moments were the reason I kept breathing.

In her home, we felt seen and cared for a little while. Loved.

But we had been trained well. So we never told her the truth.

And honestly, we weren't even sure what the truth was.

When you live in such vulnerable conditions, you don't see the whole picture—you only see what you need to survive. Pain becomes normal. Silence becomes a strategy. Confusion becomes home.

The parents who gave birth to me sent me away. The adoptive parents, who were supposed to be my shelter, felt distant and unreachable. And the sponsoring parents who promised opportunity and care met us instead with cruelty and control.

It was hard to name what was happening. Was this neglect? Was it abuse? Was this just how life should be when you depend on someone else's mercy?

Sometimes, we'd visit The Other Family in their new home. I always hesitated. I knew it upset the sponsoring parents, and their fury was a fire I didn't want to stoke. But the choice was between two kinds of discomfort, and most of the time, I chose to go.

One evening, as we sat in their apartment, a tornado struck. The rental complex was a small building with two floors—five one-bedroom units on the bottom and five more on the top. People of all ages, from different backgrounds and ethnicities, called those cramped apartments home. The wind roared like an angry beast, ripping the roof clean off the building. In the aftermath, debris lay scattered, walls torn open to the sky. The Red Cross arrived, offering food and aid to those displaced.

Mrs. Fields spent the entire weekend tirelessly and restlessly helping the extended family of her beloved students. I watched, in awe, as people around her praised her kindness and unwavering generosity. But she wasn't just the teacher who taught me well. She was a human being who exceeded expectations, giving more of herself than anyone could have imagined. That weekend, my admiration for her grew a thousand-fold, not for what she did in the classroom but for who she was—someone who made a difference in my life simply by being there when it mattered most.

But back in the sponsoring parents' house, there was no kindness left. With The Other Family gone, the sponsoring dad needed a new target for his rage. And now, it was us. I learned to move like a ghost in that house— silent, invisible. I avoided making unnecessary sounds, careful not to draw attention to myself. As always, there was no reason or rhythm to these fights, so as much as you think you would do everything possible to avoid those fights, it doesn't work that way.

An abuser who is unhappy with their own life often seeks control over others to compensate for their feelings of powerlessness and dissatisfaction.

They project their inner turmoil onto those around them, creating chaos and suffering from asserting dominance, feeding their ego, or distract themselves from their own failures. Making others miserable becomes a twisted source of validation—proof that they still hold influence, even if it's only through fear and manipulation.

The fights between my adoptive dad and the sponsoring dad grew worse. Shouting turned to threats. My adoptive dad, in one of his desperate outbursts, declared he would take us back to India.

For seven straight days, he refused to eat. A protest, a demand.

"Send me back. I want to go home."

It should have been a relief. If we left, the nightmare would finally end. But deep inside me, something twisted at the thought of returning. I wondered if I would be welcomed back with open arms or if I'd be seen as a failure. I questioned whether I would live with my adoptive parents or my biological ones—both options felt uncertain, and neither felt like home.

Along with countless encounters of violence and abuse, there were moments in my life that I will never forget, events that should never have happened, but did, and I was left with nothing but silence to carry them.

One Saturday, I was lying in bed, my long-braided hair cascading down the side, falling almost to the floor. Mummy had carefully nurtured and protected it for years, symbolizing her love and care. But that day, while I was asleep, without warning, the sponsor's daughter took scissors and cut it. She didn't ask. She didn't care. She simply snipped away at something that was mine, something sacred to me. The adults around me told me not to make a fuss and to keep quiet, so I did. I stayed silent, my heart breaking with every snip, knowing my hair, my identity, was taken from me without my consent.

Then, another time, I was sitting in the corridor, waiting for the bus. It was just a few minutes before I had to leave, and I was trying to gather myself. The sponsor's daughter approached me and ordered, "Tie my shoes." She didn't ask, she commanded. I said, "No," because I felt I wasn't being treated respectfully. But she didn't care. She kicked me hard with her boots right below my ribs. The pain was immediate—a sharp, agonizing burn that left me doubled over, wincing in pain. A huge bruise appeared on my side, and the adults again dismissed it. It didn't matter. I was just supposed to take it, to endure.

The last incident was just as painful, though in a different way. One night, during another one of their adult arguments, I was caught in it. They were pushing and shoving each other, their violence spilling over, and I became an unintended victim.

The shove came during one of their fights—a sudden burst of violence that sent me crashing to the floor. My arm twisted beneath me, the pain sharp and immediate. By morning, it had swollen into a mottled purple mess, tender to the touch. But no one asked about it. No one iced it or wrapped it in bandages. The bruise might as well have been invisible, though the ache pulsed through me for days.

Mrs. Fields noticed. She always noticed. That day, her eyes lingered on how I cradled my arm close to my body and how I winced when the sleeve brushed against my skin. "P.E. accident," I mumbled before she could ask. She studied me for a long moment, but all she said was, "Let's get you to the nurse." No probing questions, no skeptical frown—just the quiet press of her hand against my back as she guided me down the hall.

Sometimes, I wonder if she knew. Maybe it was how my voice cracked on the lie, or how I couldn't quite meet her gaze. Or perhaps she simply understood that some truths are too heavy for a child to speak aloud. Whatever the reason, she gave me the gift of silence, wrapping her concern in actions instead of words.

Over time, her glances grew more deliberate. She watched the way we hesitated before speaking, how our laughter never quite reached our eyes. She'd ask carefully if everything was alright at home. But we were experts at evasion by then—masters of the hollow smile and the rehearsed answer. For months, we endured. We folded into ourselves, shrinking beneath the weight of things we couldn't name.

"Never let anyone steal your peace."

Almost Goodbye

Nine months had passed since I arrived in the U.S. Now, at the end of ninth grade, I stood on stage at the school's award ceremony, clutching a certificate of honor and an award for academic excellence. The applause echoed around me, loud and enthusiastic, but it felt hollow—like the distant murmur of a world I no longer belonged to.

My eyes scanned the audience, searching desperately for someone who belonged to me and would meet my gaze with pride and love. The only familiar face was Mrs. Fields. She sat among the sea of strangers, beaming at me, her claps filled with genuine joy. I held onto that moment, momentarily letting it fill the aching void in my chest.

Back home in India, Mummy had never missed a single award function or cultural event. She had always been there—her presence was a quiet reassurance that I was seen and mattered. But here, standing on that stage, I felt the weight of her absence like a stone pressing against my ribs. I hadn't realized how much her presence had anchored me until now, when I stood alone, with no one but a kind teacher to celebrate me.

We often overlook the value of what we have until it's gone. Even the smallest absence can leave a startling void.

That ceremony was supposed to be a moment of triumph. Instead, it was a cruel reminder of everything I had lost. I had achieved the highest academic honor of the year, but it felt meaningless.

What was the point of success if I had no one to share it with? Awards and accomplishments meant nothing without love and family.

That lesson would stay with me for a lifetime—people always matter more than achievements, money, or anything else.

I went home partly happy, partly feeling homesick.

But that evening, the first step toward our return to India was taken.

In her kindness, Mrs. Fields gave me a parting gift that would change everything. I believe (although I'm not sure) she reported our situation to the authorities. That night, a social worker appeared at our door, leaving behind a note: they'd be returning soon.

Panic swept through the house like a wildfire.

The sponsoring parents were furious. Their rage crackled in the air, their words sharp with accusation. They blamed my adoptive sibling and me for being ungrateful and for bringing this upon the family. The house, already suffocating with tension, became a pressure cooker of whispered threats and rehearsed lies.

We were instructed on exactly what to say, what not to say, where to sit, and how to act. We practiced our roles like actors in a cruel play, learning to smile through fear.

The Other Family was summoned, and many late-night discussions occurred. It was strange to see that the sponsoring parents and The Other Family all bonded over our misery.

Soon enough, the day of the visit arrived. For one hour, we became a perfect, loving family. My sponsoring dad, who rarely smiled, was filled with laughter and warmth. My sponsoring mom, usually unpredictable and erratic, was composed and gracious—even my adoptive parents, who had barely acknowledged our existence, transformed into doting guardians. We were flawless.

The social worker took extensive notes and left, seemingly satisfied. We didn't hear back from the authorities, but the visit left the sponsoring parents spiraling. They were restless, staying up late into the night and whispering about what might happen next. Fear settled over them, thick and suffocating. They were worried. Not about us, but about themselves. And then, the decision was made. We were leaving.

The announcement came without warning. "You're going back to India. Tomorrow."

It felt like a punishment, a sentence handed down without appeal. My breath caught in my throat. I wanted to talk to my parents back home, hear their voices, and find reassurance that I hadn't ruined everything. But I wasn't allowed.

Suitcases were thrown open. Clothes were stuffed inside haphazardly. It didn't feel like travel—it felt like they were shipping us out of the country, a desperate attempt to erase us, to make it seem like we had never been here.

I sat in a daze, my heart pounding against my ribs. I had failed. I must have said too much. I must have done something wrong. And now, I was being sent back—not as a daughter who had made her parents proud, but as a burden—a failure.

My sponsoring mother was in the primary bedroom, her voice carrying through the thin walls as she paced back and forth. Her words were sharp, laced with frustration, and I could hear her husband in the living room, his low murmurs blending with the tension in the air. They were regretting it—all of it. The endless paperwork, the hoops they'd jumped through to bring us here, the favors they'd called in from other family members to co-sponsor us when their sponsorship had nearly barred our entry.

The weight of their regret hung heavy in the house, a silent storm brewing beneath the surface.

Out of nowhere, I heard, "Sushmitha," a voice cut through the tension, sharp and commanding. "Come here."

I hesitated for a moment, then obeyed, my footsteps soft against the floor. She held out the phone to me, her expression unreadable. "Here," she said, her tone clipped. "Talk to him."

A distant relative—someone older than my grandfather—wanted to speak with me. He was a man I had only heard about in passing, a prominent figure in family stories. I didn't know what to expect, but I clung to the hope that maybe, just maybe, he would offer comfort.

Maybe he wanted to know how we were doing, what had happened to us over the past few months. Maybe he would offer reassurance, his voice steady and kind, thinking of his own children and the mistakes they might have made. Maybe he would ask the questions no one else had dared to ask—why the sponsoring parents were so worried about social services, what had really happened in this house.

But the moment he spoke, that hope shattered.

"Do you think you are a big shot?" His voice was cold, dripping with disdain. "Ungrateful."

The words hit like a slap. My fingers clenched around the phone.

I had expected kindness, or at least understanding. Instead, I was met with scorn. In that instant, something inside me hardened. This man, this so-called elder, meant nothing to me. I didn't care what he thought. He had lost my respect and any power his words might have held over me.

But the weight of failure was unbearable.

I was influenced by too many Bollywood movies, where tragic endings seemed poetic, and failures met their fate with finality. That night, I made a decision.

I swallowed every pill I had brought from India—medicines for headaches, fever, nausea. I didn't know if it would work, but I wanted to end this misery.

It didn't.

Instead, I was writhing on the floor, my stomach twisting in agony. I threw up violently, my body rejecting my attempt to turn things around. The house was filled with worry for a few hours, but by morning, I was fine.

The pills had left me hollow—a raw, trembling shell of myself. My body ached, my mind was fogged, and my throat burned with the ghost of poison. And yet, even then, there was no reprieve.

My sponsoring mom, eager to clear the house for her whispered schemes, sent us away under the guise of "fresh air." My abuser needed no convincing. He herded us into the car, my sobs the only protest as we drove—not toward solace, but toward his empty house.

Every bump in the road sent fresh waves of pain through me, but worse was the terror clawing at my chest. I was trapped, weak, and utterly at his mercy—except mercy was never part of his vocabulary. He saw only opportunity.

Inside, he parked my adoptive sibling in front of a blaring TV, waiting until his eyes drooped shut. Then his hands were on me again, his breath hot against my ear. I froze, tears streaming silently, my body too broken to fight back. He didn't see a child. He didn't see suffering. He saw only his hunger.

Adoptive sibling stirred just in time—but not before his fingers began their familiar, sickening crawl.

When he returned us home, I was far more broken than when I left with him, but I was fine.

Fine enough to board the flight. Fine enough to face my failure.

Before we left, they stripped us of everything – our green cards, our Social Security cards. They wanted to erase all evidence that we had ever been in the U.S. to ensure we could never return. They wanted to make sure we never returned.

I cried the entire flight home.

When we were sent back, it wasn't about us.

The sponsoring parents only thought of themselves—their kids, their reputation, the inconvenience this investigation might bring. We were just a problem that needed to disappear, a loose thread threatening to unravel their carefully woven lives. They weren't worried about what would happen to us once we left, only about how much easier things would be for them when we were gone.

Our adoptive parents? They were too exhausted to care. The constant fights, the tension, the impossible balancing act—it had drained them. They had reached their limit. Maybe, deep down, they believed this was for the best. Perhaps they just wanted peace.

And us?

What would happen to us once we landed back home? Would we have a future, or had this journey been for nothing? Would we be seen as failures? Would there be a life to return to at all? Fear settled deep in our bones, twisting in our stomachs, but no one asked what we felt. No one wondered what would become of us.

We were just being sent back. And that was all that mattered to them.

Somewhere in mid-air, the sponsoring parents made a cold, emotionless phone call to my parents.

"We sent them back," they said and hung up the phone.

I was not a parcel. I was a battered human being, sent back like discarded luggage.

When we landed, Daddy was there.

His eyes widened in shock as he took in my appearance. The daughter he had sent away was unrecognizable. I had lost nearly 50 pounds; my once-sturdy frame was now fragile, my skin clinging to my bones. He didn't say much, but his silence was loud. It was filled with grief, with the pain of a parent who had trusted the wrong people.

We returned home, and when Mummy saw me, she also knew instantly.

She had sensed something was wrong over the months—through our phone calls, the hesitation in my voice, the way I had tried to mask my pain. But now, seeing me, she realized the truth was far worse than she had imagined.

Later, she would describe it as looking at a body with "barely any life left."

She hugged me, but I couldn't bring myself to hold on. I felt unworthy of their love and concern. I was disgusted with myself.

But my body knew long before my mind could catch up. It had held on all this time, but it finally gave way in their arms. The severe malnutrition I had endured caught up with me, and my body collapsed, weak and broken. I had to be treated immediately, to bring me back to health.

Then came the questions.

"What happened?"

The answer was simple: "Your daughter was too close to Mrs. Fields. She said too much."

That was it. That was the explanation they were given. And just like that, the blame was placed on me. Not on the sponsoring parents, not on the abuse, not on the suffering I had endured.

On me.

I had "ruined" everything.

No one asked why social services had been involved in the first place, and no one asked what had been done to me that made them so afraid of the authorities.

In desperation, Mummy and Daddy begged the sponsoring parents to take me back. They called other family members, asking if they would take me in. They even made me call Mrs. Fields, hoping she would find a way for us to return. She politely declined.

Nothing worked.

Each rejection was another nail in the coffin of their hopes. And with every plea, I felt my worth diminish further.

I spent my nights curled up, arms wrapped around my knees, sobbing silently, making sure no one could hear.

For a few days, we all stayed at a relative's place. My adoptive family, my biological parents, were digesting all of this, and there were no discussions about what the living arrangements would be next. One morning, I was packed up and brought back home to our village with Mummy and Daddy while my adoptive parents stayed behind at the relative's place.

I was at home, but I had never felt more lost.

Even in my own house, hunger felt like a crime. I hesitated before stepping into the kitchen and reaching for food, but starving felt easier.

At times, the thought of returning to my abusers seemed more bearable than staying in the safety of my own home.

Because at least with them, I knew what to expect.

Nine months ago, they sent her away like a bride—dressed in borrowed hope, carrying the weight of their expectations. Now, she returned, broken. Not stronger, not wiser, just defeated. The new life they had forced upon her had cracked her open, and she could not—would not—endure it.

But home was no refuge. Only debt, shame, and the whispers of a society that demanded answers. "Why couldn't she adjust? Why did she fail? What happened?" She was a disgrace now, a question mark in a world that only respected full stops.

"God has big plans for you. Believe it."

Part B

A Life in Motion

Being back in India, home, didn't feel comforting. It wasn't the home I had longed for over the past nine months. I had imagined that I would finally be at peace once I returned, wrapped in the warmth of my parents' embrace. But that moment never arrived. I desperately wanted to collapse into Mummy's arms and let the dam of my emotions burst open. I wanted Daddy to hold me, to tell me everything would be okay. But they couldn't. There was no time to grieve, no time to process everything I had endured. The clock was ticking, and I had to focus on what was next. How would I get back to the United States? Was it even possible without the support of my sponsoring parents? The questions consumed me and my parents, filling every moment with fear and uncertainty.

Legally, we still had the right to live and work in the U.S. Our visas and Social Security numbers were valid. But we didn't know that at the time.

For months, my parents pleaded with the sponsoring parents, begging them to take us back or at least return our documents. Every attempt was met with cold rejection. It felt like a door slammed in our faces, locking us out of both worlds—India and America.

In that day and age, a bride sent to her husband's home is expected to endure. Even if his hands bruise her arms or his family's words cut deeper than knives, she must bend like bamboo in the storm. Should the suffering become unbearable, and she flees back to her parents' house? They will open their doors to shamefully bow their heads before sending her back. Honor does not live in her safety or happiness but in her ability to remain where tradition placed her. To stay is virtue; to leave is failure that stains the entire family.

My parents belonged to that fading world - where daughters were raised to swallow their pain, where empty pockets made pride a luxury they couldn't afford. They had sold jewelry, taken loans, and mortgaged their dignity to send me across oceans once. When I returned, their trembling hands weren't just clutching at my sponsoring parents' feet - they were grasping at the last shreds of their worth in a society that measured respect in a woman's silence.

Today's girls walk differently. Education straightens their spines; paychecks fortify their voices. They know their worth and demand it. But my parents? They only knew the crushing arithmetic of debt and duty, where a daughter's suffering counted less than the village's whispers.

I hated my parents for begging.

But most of all, I hated them – the people who had taken us in and promised us a future, only to strip us of everything and cast us aside.

Then, in what felt like a twist of fate, a solution appeared. A family friend—a stranger, really—agreed to become our guardian. He lived in Ohio, working as a software engineer and sharing a small apartment with a colleague.

With his assurance, we prepared to leave once more—my adoptive mother, my adoptive sibling, and me. He told us we could still travel if our passports had valid visa stampings. No one could say for sure if it were true.

But we had no other choice.

Once again, Mummy packed our suitcases with whatever little we had left. We didn't need new clothes – we had long outgrown the luxury of wanting – but we stocked up on groceries, hoping to contribute to the household of this man we had never met.

This time, saying goodbye didn't get any easier.

The flight to Ohio was uneventful, but my heart pounded. Would we be let through? Would immigration question us? Would traveling without a green card be an issue?

But it worked.

Immigration accepted our visa stampings instead of green cards, and we were back in the United States.

Our new guardian picked us up from the airport and drove us to his apartment. It was small—just two bedrooms. The three of us shared one room while he and his roommate occupied the other. We all shared a single bathroom.

It was nothing like the spacious home of our sponsoring parents in Texas.

But we didn't need a big space; we just needed a safe one. We also needed an accessible kitchen with food.

And for that, we were grateful.

Before I left India, our family had scraped together just enough money to cover three months of expenses. Every last rupee was handed over to our guardian for safekeeping. And then, the hunt began – the search for jobs, the search for schools, the search for stability.

We applied for our green cards and Social Security cards immediately. My new school was two miles away, accessible by city bus.

Thankfully, we found jobs right away.

A small Indian restaurant owned by a South Indian couple gave us a chance. My adoptive mother worked full-time in the kitchen, while my adoptive sibling and I worked part-time on weekends.

We worked hard.

My adoptive mother washed dishes, chopped vegetables, and prepped ingredients. I worked the front—taking orders, cleaning tables, scrubbing floors, and mopping bathrooms.

The restaurant owners—Hari Uncle and Chef Aunty—were more than just employers. They were generous. They ensured we never went hungry, sending us home every night with leftovers.

Thanks to them, food was abundant during this period of my life. Although it was a vegetarian restaurant, I enjoyed its simple cooking and fell in love with making and eating Dosas, crepes made with rice and lentil batter with a side of peanut chutney and Sambar.

I was treated as a child and experienced normalcy at school. This time, I submitted my transcripts from India—something I hadn't been allowed to do in Texas—and was placed in the 11th grade instead of the 10th.

I willed myself to like American food. I ate chicken but avoided beef and pepperoni. Free breakfast and lunch to help low-income families helped me, and it was one less thing to worry about.

It wasn't easy juggling school and work, but I felt something close to freedom. I no longer lived in fear of abuse or starvation.

I often spoke to my parents in India now that I have my phone and can afford to buy cards for minutes. No longer was anyone listening in or controlling when and how I could reach them.

But I never shared any struggles with them.

What was the point?

They couldn't fix it. I refused to burden them with my pain.

Life in Ohio was a blur of responsibilities. Every new day demanded hard work.

Pay bills. Stay in school.

I didn't have the luxury of thinking about the future. College education felt like a distant dream, something I would get back to "someday."

The only reason I even stayed in high school was fear.

The U.S. had compulsory education laws under the "No Child Left Behind" policy. The guardian told us that if I dropped out, my adoptive mother could face legal consequences. It wasn't ambition that kept me going—it was the fear of what would happen if I didn't. That decision became a saving grace for my life.

We stayed with our guardian for a few months. Initially, he wasn't cruel, but his temper simmered beneath the surface. He was unpredictable, especially during phone calls with his wife back in India. We'd hear him yelling from behind closed doors, hurling cuss words, his voice thick with frustration and emotion.

We stayed out of the way.

That tension—raised voices, sharp tones, emotional chaos—was too familiar, too close after what we had endured in the sponsoring parents' house in Dallas. Even the slightest crack in someone's calm felt like a warning. We had learned to tread lightly, to shrink ourselves in the presence of volatility. Peace felt fragile, and we were afraid to breathe too loudly if it shattered.

At fifteen, I was supporting myself. I was sending money back to India, helping my parents pay off the debts they had incurred—twice—to send me to the U.S.

It was a burden I hadn't chosen. But it was mine to bear. Too much responsibility. Too much silence.

And somewhere along the way, I lost something I could never get back: The luxury of a true childhood.

"Don't hate yourself because of others."

Comfort in Chaos

In Ohio, something beautiful happened—I found a little corner of the world that finally felt like home.

The neighborhood I became part of was a vibrant patchwork of cultures, predominantly families from across Asia—Bangladesh, Pakistan, Afghanistan, and beyond. There was a rhythm to life there, a hum of activity and connection that wrapped around me like a soft shawl. The smell of home-cooked meals spilled into the streets, spices dancing through the air.

The warmth wasn't just from the food; it also came from the people. They welcomed me without hesitation, without needing explanations. No one asked for a backstory; they opened their doors and made space at their tables.

Many of the parents worked long hours at grocery stores, restaurants, and gas stations, but no matter how tired they were, they still showed up with gentle smiles and food to share. Families grew vegetables in their backyards—lush tomatoes, okra, and green chilies—and neighbors traded produce like treasure.

It was simple, generous, and rich with meaning. Most of them were Muslim, and though they came from different countries, Eid brought them together like a great, joyful wave. For Eid, a group of us kids would go from house to house, stuffing ourselves with samosas, biryani, sheer kurma, and sweets that melted on our tongues. Laughter echoed in every room.

The generosity was endless. Through these friendships, I began to see people not as categories or labels but as simply humankind, resilient and full of stories and dreams.

Their struggle as immigrants mirrored mine. Their strength helped me find my own.

Evenings were the sweetest part. We'd gather around an old VCR, legs tangled in a heap of laughter and pillows, watching Bollywood movies until our eyes burned. We'd mimic the dance moves—awkward, dramatic, and completely off-beat—and collapse into giggles. We talked about the boys we had crushes on, ate chips and candy until our stomachs hurt, and stayed up too late. For them, it was just teenage fun.

For me, it was healing. In those moments, I wasn't the girl carrying trauma or heartbreak—I was just a girl, laughing, dancing, and being silly. I felt like I was reclaiming parts of my childhood, one sleepover at a time. I loved their parents, too—how they welcomed me, checked on me, ensured I had eaten, and smiled when I walked through the door. They didn't have to do any of it, but they did. Their kindness meant everything. I didn't take any of it for granted.

Those small, happy memories?

They were lifelines.

Life was a balance for most people—a mix of highs and lows, joy and struggle. But even the highs never rose high enough to catch my breath. When I thought I might come up for air, life would shove me back under, throwing another curveball before I'd recovered from the last. There were no steady stretches, no real reprieve—just brief flickers of light before the darkness swept in again.

And I didn't see the next blow coming.

When we returned to the U.S., my adoptive father didn't come with us. He had chosen to stay in India for a while, needing a break from the trauma we had endured in Texas. I often wondered why life granted him the mercy of a pause while forcing a fifteen-year-old to keep going.

But now, he was ready to return. Unbeknownst to us, my adoptive mother had spent months working behind the scenes—submitting paperwork and securing a job at the restaurant where she worked. We only learned of it when everything was finalized.

Initially, I didn't think much of it. If anything, I felt happy for my adoptive mom. No one should live far from their loved ones. She wanted us all to move out of our guardian's apartment and into a new place.

The plan made sense. But our guardian didn't see it that way. He felt betrayed, furious that my adoptive mother had made these arrangements without consulting him. His anger turned possessive—he demanded that my adoptive sibling and I stay with him while she moved out alone.

It made no sense. We weren't a traditional family, but I wasn't about to abandon the only people I had left. I refused, and my adoptive sibling had no choice but to follow.

History repeated itself. The rage and the need for control were the same as our sponsoring parents in Texas. I had seen this before.

The need to control others is one of the cruelest things we can do. It comes from fear—fear of loss, being left behind, and not being enough. But love isn't about holding on too tightly. It's about giving people space to grow, trusting that they'll return, not out of obligation, but out of choice.

Our guardian didn't understand that.

His anger began to unravel in violent threads—verbal assaults, drunken rants, and late-night pounding on our bedroom door. The terror I thought I had escaped in Texas came crashing back, flooding the fragile sense of peace I was beginning to rebuild.

These were our last days in his home, but they felt like walking barefoot over shattered glass. He yelled whenever he found the energy, and we never yelled back.

Maybe that's why it never turned into a full-blown fight, but that didn't make it any less cruel. Other times, he screamed into the phone, but every insult was really meant for us. "Ungrateful" became a word that echoed so often in our ears that it felt stitched into my identity.

We stopped eating at home.

Thankfully, by then, we were working at a restaurant. At least we didn't have to relive the ache of starvation—we could eat what we could sneak in between shifts. But even after we moved into a small apartment, the nightmare followed us.

He would show up drunk, banging on our door, hurling slurred threats into the dark. We stopped answering, but he didn't stop coming.

We didn't think to call 911 or even know if we could. A twisted sense of obligation kept us silent. After all, hadn't he helped us? Hadn't he taken us in? Our silence was a currency we paid with shame.

The final blow came when he refused to return the $11,000 we had brought from India, along with every single dollar we had managed to save since. It was a devastating loss.

I was earning only $5 an hour. That money came from a family that had already gone into debt—twice—to send me here.

The night terrors returned, and sleep became a battleground again. My body remembered what I tried so hard to forget. But when it felt like the darkness might swallow me whole, a light appeared.

Uma, a bank manager at a local credit union, and her husband, Jay, entered our lives like an answered prayer. They were an Indian couple without children, but they poured all their love into their two dogs—and, eventually, into us.

Uma Aunty, as I fondly called her, was a force of nature: strong, sharp, and unshakable. Her voice carried authority, and her presence demanded respect. Jay Uncle was her opposite—gentle and soft-spoken. Together, they became a part of our broken family.

We met them through the restaurant owners, and when Uma Aunty learned of our situation, she didn't hesitate. She stepped in with a ferocity that sent the guardian running. She made it clear: his reign of terror was over. My adoptive sibling, still clinging to the hope of pacifying him, continued visiting him in secret. But after Uma Aunty intervened, we cut ties completely. I was finally able to exhale a sigh of relief.

Uma Aunty didn't stop at saving us; she taught us how to rebuild. She helped us open bank accounts, guiding us toward financial independence. She checked in on us, brought us small gifts, and treated us as if we mattered.

For one of my birthdays, she gave me her mother's earrings, a touching gesture and a token of love. Spending time with her felt like being wrapped in a warm blanket on the coldest night—a reminder that kindness still existed.

I made it through eleventh grade, balancing school and work. Every day was a tightrope walk with no safety net and no room to slip. There were no sports teams, clubs, or carefree luxuries that usually color a teenager's world.

Weekends belonged to the restaurant. My feet throbbed from standing for hours; the physical toll was easier to bear than the quiet, constant ache inside me—the one that longed for love, for comfort, for someone to notice how hard I was trying.

Weekdays were just as relentless. After school, I rushed to my second job at a pizza place, where I scrubbed dishes, wiped down tables, and smiled through exhaustion.

I came home at night too worn out to think, let alone feel. Homework happened wherever I could fit it—in the library between classes, during lunch breaks, or at work if no one was looking.

Every hour of my day was claimed. Every moment served a purpose.

"One beautiful heart is better than a thousand beautiful faces."

The Breaking Again

 Hope is as inevitable as spring.

Even after the most brutal winter, spring always finds a way to return. So does hope. It's stitched into our very nature—to hope, even when there's no reason to, even when everything hurts. Slowly, I began to hope again, not for miracles, grand gestures, or happy endings.

Just for a simple matter.

An uneventful life. A life with no abuse, no yelling, no fights, no starvation. Just hard work. Just peace.

The nightmare with the guardian felt like a closed chapter. The shadows felt less menacing.

There was immense pride in knowing we no longer lived under an abusive authority—no sponsoring parents looming over us, no guardian dictating our every move.

We had earned our freedom with sweat, exhaustion, and defiance, trading long hours of labor for the right to live on our own terms. The physical strain of working without breaks felt justified. The pain in my feet and the fatigue in my bones—it all seemed like a small price to pay.

The $11,000 we had entrusted to him was surely gone—swallowed by his greed, lost to his betrayal. No amount of pleading or reasoning could bring it back.

We had to start over. And we did, with the help of our generous restaurant owners. They knew our struggles, though we never spoke of them in detail. They slipped us meals when business was slow. Hari Uncle, a soft-hearted man, drove us home each night. His wife, one of the hardest-working women I have witnessed, would pack leftovers for us in small plastic containers, pretending it was to "clear the fridge."

Rebuilding our lives was slow, but we felt hopeful. A few days after we moved into our new apartment, my adoptive father arrived from India. Unlike before, when we came to live with the sponsoring parents, my adoptive parents felt hopeful for their future. Working at the restaurant had given my adoptive mother a glimpse of what they could build for themselves: a sense of self-worth from honest, hard-earned wages. After my adoptive father returned, he joined her at the same restaurant.

We didn't own a car, so we learned to rely on public transportation for grocery shopping, errands, and even getting to work. Most days, we walked. A mile or two didn't faze us; it became part of our rhythm. But winters in Ohio were unforgiving. The cold bit through our layers and icy sidewalks made each step a struggle. Sometimes, the restaurant owners offered us a ride. It might've seemed like a small gesture to them, but it meant the world to us. A brief break from the freezing wind, a small act of kindness that helped us hold on a little longer.

Slowly, with each saved dollar and shift worked, the towering mountain of debt back home began to feel just a little less impossible to climb. Still, it loomed—ever present, casting a long shadow over every step forward. But I kept walking anyway, driven by duty, hope, and sheer will.

Yet even as I found ways to survive, I remained untethered—drifting between households, expectations, and relationships that never felt like mine.

While we tried to build something that resembled a home, it quickly became clear that what we had wasn't a family—it was a fragile truce held together by politeness and distance.

My adoptive parents weren't unkind. They were polite, cordial, and even generous at times. But they didn't know how to be parents. They couldn't love me as a daughter, and I never truly felt like their child.

Living with them was like sharing a train compartment with strangers. If someone stumbled, you might exchange a few words, nod, or show a small kindness.

But when the journey ends, you part ways without a second thought. Maybe that's how they saw me—just a traveler passing through. Someone they were obligated to accompany for a stretch of the ride, nothing more.

The weight of parenting was too much for them—too complex, too honest. What existed between us wasn't love. It didn't belong. It was a quiet, mutual understanding of roles neither of us chose, but both were stuck. They weren't my safe place, and I wasn't their daughter.

So, while my friends fussed over SAT scores, college applications, and dorm room plans, I was silently watching from the sidelines, unsure if the world had a door open for someone like me.

I kept my grades up. Teachers praised me and encouraged me to reach higher. They believed in a future I wasn't sure I could imagine. College felt like a luxury reserved for someone else's daughter—someone with a parent helping them fill out forms, walking campus tours, offering a safety net.

I went to the workshops. I picked up the brochures. I tried to believe I belonged in those conversations. But I was alone in it. In my world, college wasn't a rite of passage—it was a privilege. And deep down, I didn't think I was meant for that privilege.

I was meant to clock in at restaurants. To hustle. To survive. If I dared to have them, dreams had to stay within reach—small enough not to disappoint me when they went unfulfilled. Because college wasn't for girls like me, it was for the ones with someone to help them dream.

When I thought the nightmare with our Ohio guardian was behind us, it roared back one night. He showed up at our door, breath reeking of alcohol, eyes wild with bitterness.

We hesitated, unsure of what to expect. Then, in an instant, he lunged at my adoptive father, hands clawing like a predator's, voice a guttural roar that shook the walls.

Shouts. Shoves. The sickening thud of fists meeting flesh.

I stood frozen, my heart pounding as his rage filled the air like a toxic fog.

Every second stretched unbearably long, fear wrapping around my chest like a vice.

Finally, after a brutal struggle, he stormed out, slamming the door so hard that the walls trembled.

Silence followed, thick and suffocating. We stood there, shaken, breathless, the weight of fear settling deep in our bones.

That night, I crawled into bed with a heart like a stone in my chest, dread whispering in the back of my mind. What if this wasn't over?

The next morning, we called Uma Aunty from the restaurant. Her voice was calm but firm. She promised to come after work.

When she arrived, my adoptive parents were at the restaurant, leaving just the two of us. We sat in the living room, with natural light filtering through the window and afternoon shadows stretching across the floor. She looked at me with steady eyes, and the truth spilled out.

My adoptive sibling had been revisiting the guardian. Fear and frustration tangled inside me as I admitted it. My voice trembled. Uma Aunty's face darkened. I wasn't there to see what happened next, but I could picture it—her storming into his workplace, confronting him, ensuring he knew this had to stop. She wasn't the kind of woman to stay silent in the face of injustice.

I attempted to push the day's events aside that evening, a rare evening off from work. A friend came over to do homework. We laughed a little and shared notes, and for a brief moment, I felt normal. She left around 6:30 PM, and I ran out and bought some personal items—soap, deodorant, shampoo—Dove products.

Purchasing those felt like a luxury, an upgrade. By the time I returned home, it was 9:00 PM.

The apartment was silent; my adoptive mom was in the bedroom lying down.

I took a long shower, letting the steam and my newly purchased products wash over me. The small act of self-care felt indulgent, almost rebellious. The first time I showered with Dove products—shampoo, conditioner, body wash, and that soft-scented body spray—I felt like I had stepped into someone else's life—someone wealthier. Someone loved.

I poured the shampoo into my hand, and its silky texture and gentle lather made me feel like I was doing something indulgent. The conditioner smoothed my tangled hair with ease, and for once, I didn't feel like I had to fight with it. The body wash, thick and creamy, glided over my skin like a blanket. I closed my eyes and breathed in its sweet, clean, and soft scent. It smelled like safety, like comfort.

Afterward, I sprayed the Dove body mist under my shirt, the cool mist settling on my skin like a secret. I didn't have expensive things, but this felt close.

With wet hair, I warmed up some leftovers from the fridge and ate in the living room in front of the old TV we had salvaged from the apartment trash. Someone had left it outside, abandoned, but it was a treasure to us.

It had a built-in VCR. We had no cable, but my adoptive sibling would sometimes rent cassettes. One was lying there. I didn't care what it was—I just wanted to watch for a bit mindlessly. So, I pressed play. The screen flickered to life, filling the empty room with voices, laughter, and stories that weren't mine.

Then the door opened.

My adoptive sibling walked in, still in his White Castle uniform. The smell of fried oil, cheeseburgers, and sweat clung to him. But his eyes—bloodshot, burning with fury—sent ice through my veins. Something was wrong.

He started yelling, and I understood that Uma Aunty had visited him that evening. Before I could speak, he lunged.

His fists crashed into my face and body, knocking the air from my lungs.

Pain exploded everywhere.

I tried to scream, but no sound came.

I was barely five feet tall and weighed just 100 pounds. He was almost six feet, lean but strong. I never stood a chance.

My adoptive mother rushed in, screaming, trying to pull him away. She wasn't strong enough. He hit me again. And again. And again.

I curled into a ball, arms wrapped around my head, waiting for it to stop. The fear paralyzed me more than the pain. I knew why this was happening.

Uma Aunty had gone to his workplace. She had confronted him.

And now, I was paying the price.

He knew I couldn't fight back.

He knew I wouldn't call the police—because not calling the police had become the theme of our lives.

In the sponsor's home, when terror unfolded behind closed doors, a police officer lived right next door with his family. All we had to do was walk over and ring the bell.

But somewhere along the way, I learned that enduring abuse was a sign of gratitude. That enduring abuse was what made a family.

And he knew that.

He knew there would be no consequences.

So he kept going.

Pouring every ounce of his rage into me until he was too exhausted to continue.

Then, without a word, he left.

The door slammed.

Silence.

I lay there, bruised and broken, gasping for air.

Hours later, I dragged myself to bed.

My body throbbed with pain, and my face was so swollen that I could barely recognize my reflection.

The next morning, I picked up the phone, my hands trembling.

I called my parents in India.

The moment Daddy answered, my voice broke.

I started sobbing uncontrollably. He asked me, "What happened? Ammulu, what's wrong?"

I gathered myself and told him everything.

Every blow.

Every moment of terror.

His voice cracked with anguish. But what could he do? He was thousands of miles away. His hands were tied the day he signed those adoption papers.

He had lost the right to protect me.

And I had lost the comfort of knowing someone would always have my back.

Throughout this book, you'll notice something.

I never call my adoptive sibling "brother."

That word carries a weight I've carried in my heart for years—a longing I've never been able to fulfill.

As an only child, I grew up watching my best friend with her older brother. I saw how he teased her, protected her, and was gentle with her.

I longed for that bond and would ask my parents to give me an older brother. They would laugh at my innocent request.

I dreamed of having an older brother of my own—someone who would shield me from the world's cruelty. Someone who would spoil me with affection. Someone who would rescue me when I stumbled.

I imagined a brother as my strength, my family.

He was none of those things.

The person who should have been my brother became my tormentor instead.

I try to tell myself that his pain shaped him. The abuse he endured and the stress he carried from the sponsor's home and the guardian's house must have taken a toll. The last few years of both our lives were far from normal. No adult could properly process such turmoil, let alone a child.

Abuse is a cycle because pain, when left unhealed, festers and turns into patterns—what is endured often becomes what is inflicted. But breaking the cycle requires help, money, and resources—things we never had. So, we carried it on our shoulders, the weight causing us to limp through life.

Having my adoptive sibling in my life could have been healing. We were the same age, walking the same uncertain path. Everything that happened to me had happened to him too. We carried the same wounds, the same losses. Sharing should have brought us closer, giving us a sense of understanding and comfort.

But trauma doesn't always unite. Sometimes, it destroys.

Instead of healing together, we became trapped in its cycle. His pain turned outward, making him my abuser. Mine turned inward, making me his victim. The bond that could have saved us only broke us further.

But even with that understanding, I can't give him a pass.

He doesn't get to use his fists and legs to hurt me. He doesn't get to trash me as if I were nothing.

The scars he left—visible and invisible—are proof of a bond that never existed. A relationship that failed to live up to the word I so desperately wanted to give him.

"A good life needs some bad days, too."

A New Beginning

After he left, I lay there, my body throbbing, every inch of me screaming in pain.

My face was swollen, my ribs ached with every breath. Bruises would bloom where his fists had landed—ugly, unforgiving reminders of what had just happened. I wanted to move, but even the most minor shift sent fresh waves of agony through me. The exhaustion wasn't just in my limbs; it was deeper than that, sinking into my bones, making me feel like I was drowning in it.

But the worst pain wasn't the one I could feel on my skin. It was the one inside my head.

Shame burned through me first. Was it my fault? Had I provoked him? Maybe if I had stayed quiet or seen it coming, I could have stopped it.

But then came the anger—hot and sharp, pressing against my ribs like a scream I couldn't let out. I hated him. He hated what he did. I hated that I couldn't stop it.

And then, just as quickly, fear swallowed it all, because this wouldn't be the last time.

He knew I wouldn't fight back, and he knew I wouldn't call the police because I never had. Suffering in silence meant I was part of a family.

But if this was family, why did it break me?

I felt powerless, as if I no longer belonged in my skin.

I wanted to disappear into the walls, to become so invisible that he would forget I existed. But I knew that wasn't how this worked. No matter how much I shrank, the blows would still come.

I closed my eyes, trying to will myself to sleep, pretending that when I woke up, everything would be different. But deep down, I knew the truth.

This was my life. And no one was coming to save me.

The next morning, Hari Uncle and his wife came as they always did - to pick up my adoptive mother. She invited them inside. When Hari Uncle saw me, his eyes filled with tears. He didn't say anything at first—he just stood there, staring at the bruises on my face, his whole body stiff with anger.

Then, his voice shook as he called my adopted sibling, demanding to know where he was. But the phone rang and rang. No answer. He hadn't come home after attacking me. He wasn't sorry. He wasn't afraid.

After a while, they had to leave to open the restaurant, but they told me to rest before they did.

I didn't say a word.

I couldn't.

Tears rolled down my cheeks, the salt stinging the broken skin on my face.

I was scared to stay home alone. What if he came back?

I didn't have the strength to endure another beating.

So, I went with them to the restaurant, forcing myself to work despite the pain. When I could no longer stand, I retreated to the back room, my body trembling with exhaustion.

But my heart was unwilling to heal. It was filled with questions that clawed at my mind like relentless ghosts. Why was I suffering this fate?

Why had God chosen this path for me? Why did my parents give me away? Why did the ones who adopted me never truly care for me?

Later that evening, they called Uma Aunty and told her what had happened. She came right away, her face dark with anger. But no one could erase what had already been done.

The next day, he came home. He walked through the house as if nothing had happened.

As if I hadn't spent the night before shaking in pain. As if my swollen face, my bruised ribs, my silence—none of it mattered.

And when he finally spoke to my adoptive mother a few days later, it became clear—he had rewritten the story in his mind.

The guardian had poisoned him against me, twisting the truth until he believed I was the reason our family had moved. In his mind, I had done this. I had caused it all.

To him, I was the villain. But I wasn't a villain. I wasn't some master manipulator.

I was just a girl. A girl who had been beaten. A girl who was lost in a situation she didn't understand.

Today, if someone tried to do this to me or anyone else, I wouldn't hesitate to call the police. But back then, I didn't understand that silence wasn't strength. Staying quiet didn't make me safe. It only invited more pain.

In his eyes and how he moved, I sensed a possibility of this happening again if I didn't find the strength to escape.

I witnessed as a child in my own family that if an abuser hits you once and sees that you won't fight back and do not face any repercussions, the chances of it happening again are terrifyingly high. Abuse is about power and control. If the abuser realizes they can harm you without facing the consequences, they only become bolder.

I didn't want to fight. I just wanted to get away.

I threw away every Dove product I had. *To this day, I still can't use them. The scent, look, and feel take me back to the scariest night of my life.*

A few days later, in my restlessness, I asked my friend Soniya if I could stay at her house after school. She agreed without hesitation. Her mom, Ponni Aunty, welcomed me into their home without question. They didn't live in a house or an apartment; they lived in a motel as a family, getting their footing in this country. But whatever it was, they welcomed me into it with open arms. It's not the structure that makes it a home; it's the people. And those people became my people.

We watched TV, did homework, and went to bed that night. It was a normal home. A place where parents took care of their children without expecting them to earn their keep. That night, I saw what I had longed for—the kind of love that didn't have to be earned. A glimpse of what unconditional care looked like. One night turned into a week.

A week turned into months. I quit both my jobs—the weekend shifts at the restaurant and the weekday shifts at the pizza place. Soniya's family never asked me for rent. They never expected anything in return. They treated me like their own.

If Soniya's mom picked up Taco Bell for her or KFC or KFC for her brother, she asked what I wanted, too. No hesitation. No conditions. As if I had always belonged. Soniya and I shared a room, and I slept deeply and peacefully beside her. I had forgotten what it felt like to wake up without a pit of anxiety in my stomach.

On Saturdays, we slept in, the sunlight streaming through the curtains, warming our faces. We basked in the quiet luxury of feeling safe. Some weekends, we skipped meals altogether—breakfast, lunch, dinner—staying in bed, slipping in and out of sleep, our biggest concern being what movie to watch next. This was new. Fascinating.

This is what young people are supposed to do, I thought. Go to school. Sleep long hours. Eat junk food. Watch movie marathons. Work a few hours a week to learn responsibility. Worry about simple things—what to wear, how to do their hair.

They should not worry about the next meal, abuse, or making enough money to make ends meet.

With the weight of survival no longer crushing me, I cautiously began to dream, carefully, as if my dreams were fragile things that might shatter if I reached too fast. Soniya was preparing for college, flipping through brochures, filling out applications, and talking about majors and dorm life. Watching her, I started to imagine a future for myself, too. But the thought felt foreign, like trying on someone else's clothes and expecting them to fit.

Could I belong in a classroom instead of a restaurant kitchen? Could I dream beyond just making it through another day?

I still believed dreams were a luxury for others—people with families to guide them, homes filled with love, and safety nets to catch them when they fell. I thought survival was all I could hope for; dreaming beyond my circumstances felt selfish, even foolish.

But watching Soniya plan her future and seeing her family encourage her without hesitation made me realize something: dreams weren't just for the privileged but also for me.

Everyone deserves to dream and believe in a future where happiness isn't just a distant wish but a reality. No matter how helpless the world makes us feel or how much our surroundings try to convince us we are unworthy, we must hold onto the right to define our dreams.

For too long, I let others dictate what I was allowed to want. I had handed my future over to those who only saw me as a worker, a burden, someone whose worth was measured by how much I could endure. But I wasn't put on this earth to suffer; I was meant to dream, build, and thrive.

Unlearning years of survival mode wasn't easy; allowing myself to believe that I, too, could reach for something greater took time. Yet, In that house, surrounded by the warmth of Soniya's family, I saw the first flickers of possibility.

I could envision a path where I wasn't merely struggling to make it through each day but moving toward something meaningful.

And I vowed then that I wouldn't let anyone else define my future for me ever again.

My English teacher, Mr. Bartels, became my guide in school. He taught me how to craft essays, how to structure research papers, and—most importantly—how to believe in my own potential.

He often spoke about his dreams: how he wanted to retire in Maine with his wife, how he longed to sing in a choir, spending his days surrounded by music.

Years later, I saw those dreams come to life on his Facebook page, and I was happy for him.

Inspired by his belief in me, I applied to several colleges, Colleges. The idea of leaving my past behind and starting afresh somewhere far away felt like a lifeline.

Even though I took my SATs late in my senior year, I scored well and was accepted into nearly every school I applied. My goal was clear: to move away, to carve out a new life for myself, far from the echoes of my past.

I craved distance. I wanted to leave behind yet another painful chapter of my life.

My decision to leave my adoptive parents' home wasn't sudden or dramatic; it was slow, quiet, and almost unnoticeable at first.

Initially, they got used to not seeing me on weekends, then weekdays, and eventually, I stopped coming back at all.

I didn't offer explanations. I didn't ask for permission. I let my absence speak for me—I was done.

I had no knowledge of in-state versus out-of-state tuition, so I let my heart guide me, touring colleges far from home.

The idea of starting over somewhere unfamiliar felt liberating. But reality hit quickly—out-of-state tuition was expensive, impossibly so. The numbers didn't add up, and I couldn't afford to dream unquestioningly.

Money was a struggle—not because I was reckless, but because I made minimum wage and lacked the financial literacy to manage it.

There was no money to begin with.

I stumbled through phone bills, overdraft fees, and everyday expenses. I made mistakes: missed payments, financial missteps, temporary fixes that left me feeling dishonest and ashamed, and I was scrambling to make ends meet.

I believed that a lack of money was the reason for my complicated life. If Mummy and Daddy hadn't struggled financially, they might have had the luxury to raise their child; my adoptive parents also cared more about financial gains than making a lifelong bond with me.

I refuse to live a life of scarcity again.

I thought education has always been my strength; I must make it my path to something greater. When I have children, they will never know the pain of being given up—they will grow up loved, supported, and secure. To make that future possible, I must keep pushing forward, pursuing higher education not just for myself but also for them.

I don't need to be rich, but I want to be wealthy—in stability, opportunity, and the ability to give back. I want to put food on tables, not just my own. I want to lift kids who've been made to feel 'less than' because money was tight. And when I finally have a family, I'll ensure their dreams are never limited by fear or lack.

That's why I chose pre-pharmacy. It's not just about making a decent living—though my advisor reminded me pharmacists do well—it's about building a foundation strong enough to hold up everyone who depends on me, starting with my future self.

Life doesn't pause while you wrestle with decisions; it moves forward, relentless and indifferent to inner turmoil. And in my uncertainty, prom arrived.

I didn't fully understand the significance of prom. It seemed similar to a farewell party in Indian schools—a celebration where first-year students sent off the seniors, honoring their transition into the world. I wasn't particularly attached to the idea, but Soniya was excited, and Ponni Aunty insisted I go.

I decided to wear a saree, an Indian traditional garment, elegantly draped around me. Soniya, ever radiant, wore an embellished skirt and crop top. I still wasn't comfortable with the usual prom dresses, and Ponni Aunty supported my choice without hesitation.

That night, she helped me get ready with the same care Mummy once had. She lent me a red Kanchivaram pure silk saree—rich and regal—and adorned me with traditional Indian jewelry from her collection. As she fastened the necklace around my throat, her fingers warm and steady, I felt a pang of longing.

She reminded me of Mummy.

Mummy always took her time on special occasions, ensuring I looked beautiful, fussing over every little detail with love. Standing before the mirror, draped in silk and tradition, I felt a quiet ache.

Most of my classmates arrived in pairs, and a few of us came as a group. We probably stood out in our Indian attire, but if anyone thought we looked different, we didn't notice.

That night, under the glittering lights, I danced.

With the bit of money I had left after paying for college applications, I made an impulsive decision—one that felt right in my heart, even if it didn't make sense on paper. I would go to India for the summer after graduation.

It wasn't practical. The responsible choice would have been to work, save, and prepare for college. But I was exhausted by the weight of practicality. I longed for a break, a chance to breathe, and step away from the endless pressure of being "responsible."

I knew, deep down, that Soniya's family wouldn't mind if I stayed longer. But I didn't want to overstay my welcome. I didn't want to be a burden on them.

Yet, the kindness they had shown me was overwhelming, especially Ponni Aunty. She had taught me that love wasn't something that needed to be earned—it could be given freely, without expectations. Her love was soft and constant in the way she included me in her life through little gestures that spoke volumes.

She even taught me how to make gulab jamun—sweet, golden dumplings soaked in syrup—just as her mother had once taught her. I use the same technique to this day and remember her kindness *with gratitude.*

Ponni Aunty's love wasn't loud or demanding. It was steady and straightforward—like a quiet rhythm that calmed the chaos inside me. It lived in the meals we shared, the small questions she asked to check on my well-being, and how she was just present.

As I prepared for India, I remembered where I had been. That night—the worst night of my life, the one where my body and heart took a hit—could have crushed me. But instead, I chose to turn it into a stepping stone.

That painful night didn't define me; it shaped me and propelled me forward. I was leaving for India, not just to escape but to reclaim parts of myself I thought I'd lost.

"Remember, some things have to end for better things to begin."

The Bloom

Children deserve to be nurtured, loved, and guided until they are ready to spread their wings and soar into the world. They must be taught with care, patience, and endless compassion—so that when they step into their journey, filled with responsibilities, stumble, fall, or lose their way, they always feel the unwavering embrace of their parents. A safety net that whispers, *It's okay. I've got you.*

But I… I didn't have that.

Some days, I woke up with fists clenched and my heart pounding, ready to battle the world; I kept moving, one step at a time, because standing still was never an option. But then there were days when I was so tired—not just tired of fighting but tired of surviving, tired of living, and tired of carrying the weight of a world that felt so heavy, cold, and indifferent.

When you're in survival mode, day after day, year after year, with no one to catch you when you fall, no one to hold you when you break, no one to tell you it's going to be okay… it chips away at your soul. It plants seeds of doubt, of despair, of wanting to give up. And sometimes, in the quietest, darkest moments, those seeds grow into thoughts that whisper, What's the point?

I carried those thoughts with me, even as I achieved milestones that should have felt like victories.

I graduated high school at the top of my class, a triumphant and bittersweet honor. I was chosen to speak at my graduation, and I stood at the podium, my heart racing beneath my graduation gown. I looked out at the sea of faces—teachers, classmates, families—and chose my words carefully. I spoke about time and how the younger generation could harness it wisely to achieve success.

It was a safe topic.

One that didn't reveal the scars I carried or the battles I had fought.

Looking back, I wish I had given a different speech. I wish I had talked about resilience. About the strength it takes to rise after every fall. Hope, even in the slightest flicker, can light the darkest paths. But at that time, I wasn't ready. The pain was still too raw, too close to the surface.

The family that came to support me that day wasn't my own. It was Soniya's family. They arrived with flowers, beaming with pride as they cheered me on. After the ceremony, they took me out to celebrate, their laughter wrapping around me like a warm embrace.

I was deeply honored and deeply grateful.

But still, I longed to see my parents in the crowd.

Awards and accolades meant so much to Mummy. Each one felt like a validation, proof that she was doing a good job raising me. It wasn't just a trophy or a certificate—it was her quiet way of saying, I'm succeeding as a mother. She would have clapped the loudest for my achievements. She would have been proud to watch me deliver that speech and graduate with honors.

A few days after graduation, with two suitcases and a heart full of gratitude, I said goodbye to Soniya and Ponni Aunty. I hugged them tightly, the weight of their kindness pressing into me as I boarded a Greyhound bus to the airport. From there, I was on my way to India.

I had secured college admission. I felt confident—not because I had all the answers, but because I believed I could find them.

Returning to India was like stepping into a warm embrace. I spent my days with my grandparents and parents, soaking in their love. I didn't have much money to spend, but I didn't need it. Home was enough.

There is no greater blessing than time spent with those who love you—and no love quite like that of grandparents. They doted on me endlessly, feeding me until I protested and wrapping every moment in warmth. The visit passed in what felt like a heartbeat, and suddenly, I was packing my bags again in preparation for my departure.

I slept beside Daddy those last few nights, letting his presence soothe the ache of goodbye. But somewhere along the way, I realized something had shifted: this was no longer 'my' home. It was where Mummy and Daddy lived—a place I visited but no longer belonged.

Mummy, now an expert in packing, ensured every bit of space in my suitcases was used efficiently. She filled them with food, clothes, and small comforts to carry with me into this new phase of life. The car ride to the airport was silent, except for the occasional sniffle. Saying goodbye to my aging grandparents was always the most challenging part—eyes full of tears, hearts full of love.

But just as I was about to leave, a sudden realization sent a chill down my spine.

I didn't have my green card.

Panic surged through me. Was it at my adoptive parents' house? At Soniya's? Lost somewhere along the way? I had no idea. I rifled through my bags, my hands trembling. My pulse thundered in my ears.

I still had the stamp in my passport that allowed me to travel back to the U.S.—the same one I had used when I first went to Ohio. It was still valid. I had done this before. I had proof. I reassured myself that everything would be fine.

But when I arrived at the airport in Hyderabad, the Air India staff refused to let me board.

They stared at my documents, unfamiliar with the stamp. They didn't want to take the risk.

I pleaded. Explained. I showed them everything I had.

But their answer remained firm.

Defeated, I dragged my suitcase from the airport and returned to my parents' home. The future I had carefully constructed dangled precariously, slipping through my fingers like sand.

The next day, I traveled to the U.S. consulate in Chennai, hoping to get a temporary travel letter. My hands were clammy as I held my documents, my heart pounding with desperation. This letter was my only chance. It had to work.

But my hope was short-lived.

The letter would take six weeks to arrive.

Six weeks.

Six weeks meant I would miss my freshman orientation at OSU, which meant I could no longer attend that semester. The reality of it hit like a gut punch.

I pleaded with the consulate officer, showing them my admission letter, explaining the mandatory orientation, and emphasizing how much was at stake. My voice trembled, but I refused to break.

It didn't matter. They wouldn't make an exception.

I walked out and met Daddy outside the embassy. Initially, he was relieved that there was a way, and the implications of the six weeks kicked in when I explained to him what was at stake.

Another setback. Another roadblock stopped me from getting to my destiny.

During those six weeks, my entire family was on edge. My parents, who had once sent me away in hopes of a better future and re-sent me again when I returned, now held their breath, wondering if that future had crumbled. Every time I had to board a flight back to the U.S., there were hoops to jump through and hurdles to navigate. It never came easy. It was hope the first time, persistence the second time, and patience this time.

But internally, I was crumbling. My worth, happiness, and even my very existence felt tied to my ability to return to the U.S. The pressure was suffocating, but I couldn't succumb to it. I had to stay afloat.

My carefully laid plans had shattered in an instant. I had no choice but to pivot.

I scrambled to apply to Wright State University in Dayton, Ohio, hoping I could transfer to OSU later. I already had some credits from OSU, so I imagined it wouldn't be too hard to make the switch.

It wasn't what I had planned, but it was a way forward.

When the acceptance letter arrived, I felt a flicker of relief—a small light in the overwhelming darkness. I registered for classes, holding onto the belief that this was only temporary.

Six weeks later, the travel letter finally arrived, it should have been a moment of celebration. But by then, I had been exhausted by the fight. I was drained mentally, emotionally, and physically.

When I landed in the U.S., I filed for a replacement green card.

I navigated it alone. I was exhausted. Frustrated.

I was angry at myself for not knowing better.

A single mistake had cost me time, stability, and peace of mind.

That experience taught me an invaluable lesson: life requires flexibility. Plans fall apart, circumstances shift, and clinging too tightly to expectations only leads to heartbreak.

I had to adapt.

I applied for financial aid, searched for scholarships, and secured a job on campus—all while juggling the weight of starting over. I found a room with a few other girls off campus. I didn't have the money for a deposit, but they understood.

They waited.

Eventually, things fell into place.

One semester turned into three before I transferred to Ohio State University. It wasn't what I had envisioned, but it gave me lifelong friends, unforgettable experiences, and a lesson I would carry forever.

There were days when I felt lost, confused, and overwhelmed by the enormity of figuring out the system, handling finances, and navigating adulthood.

It was hard. So incredibly hard.

But I survived.

Not because I always had support but because I learned how to hold myself up when no one else could.

That's the most challenging part – sticking with it when you feel alone when there's no one to lift you.

But if you sustain yourself long enough and push through enough challenges, the support will come. You will build a family—not always by blood, but by choice.

And one day, you will be that support for someone else.

Life has a way of coming full circle. The struggles you endure today will one day become the strength you offer to others.

And that... is what survival truly means.

"Even delays are blessings. Trust the universe."

College, Unfiltered

C.S. Lewis once said, "Hardship often prepares an ordinary person for an extraordinary destiny."

College was a challenging yet profoundly transformative chapter of my life. It was a time of discovery, a delicate dance between two worlds: the carefree joy of embracing the college experience like my roommates and the disciplined drive to excel academically. For a while, I wandered the easier path—paved with laughter, spontaneity, and midnight adventures.

There were mornings I strolled into class late, my mind still foggy from the previous night's escapades. Once, I even missed the chance to take a chemistry final because I arrived a few minutes after the test had started. Someone had already turned in their paper, and the stern and unyielding professor refused to let me take the exam.

I walked away with a C—the first of my academic life. That grade sat like a stone on my chest, a stark reminder that I was letting myself drift, that I was sabotaging my potential. It wasn't just a grade—it was a reckoning. I knew I had to shift gears, refocus, and recommit to the very thing that had brought me to this country in the first place: success.

And just when I needed it most, another kind stranger appeared. Deepu, a fellow student from India pursuing her master's degree, stepped into my life. She had a smile that could light up the darkest room, and I often told her she had a million-dollar smile. She walked alongside me, offering the support and encouragement I needed to get back on track and reminding me that I wasn't alone in this journey.

Deepu and I were both naive in our ways. She had only recently moved to the U.S., still adjusting to a new world, yet there was a steadiness about her—a quiet patience from growing up in a close-knit nuclear family. She had been raised with love, stability, and the instinct to care for others.

It was in the way she listened. The way she noticed the little things – whether I had eaten, whether I seemed off that day, or whether I just needed someone to sit beside me in silence.

On the other hand, I had spent so much of my life searching for that kind of warmth. The lack of love in my life had made me hungry for connection, for kindness that didn't come with conditions. And Deepu? She gave it so effortlessly and naturally that I couldn't help but admire her.

She took care of me in ways I didn't even know I needed—bringing me dinner from her off-campus job, introducing me to her friends, and doing my chores when I was overwhelmed. She had a way of spoiling me while also looking after me, ensuring I got a taste of the carefree youth I had never truly experienced.

"You're still young," she'd say, brushing off my protests. "You deserve to just breathe for once."

In return, I brought energy and drive to our friendship. I pushed her beyond her comfort zone and encouraged her to dream bigger, take risks, and embrace the unknown. Where she was cautious, I was impulsive. Where she hesitated, I charged ahead.

We were different, yet we complemented each other. We navigated the world together, making mistakes, learning, and growing. Through it all, we supported each other as friends and as the sisters we had chosen to be.

She quickly became more than a friend; she became a beloved sister.

Thanks to my years of working in a restaurant during high school—where I often stepped in to cook when needed—I developed quite a skill for making Indian food.

In our shared living space, cooking became my role. One roommate or Deepu would chop and prep, another would clean, and I would take charge of the kitchen. I cooked for our group of friends, for birthday parties, and even for larger gatherings.

Chicken curry was my specialty, but I made most South Indian dishes with ease. The aroma of spices, the sizzle of onions in hot oil, and the warmth of a home-cooked meal became my way of giving back.

Deepu, while searching for an on-campus job, secured me a position as a research assistant for an ethnic studies professor. This role allowed me to quit my grocery store job and focus more on my studies.

The research position paid better than my previous job and temporarily relieved my financial troubles. Financial aid covered my tuition, and my expenses became manageable with part-time work.

I applied for every scholarship I could find on campus, ensuring I maintained a strong academic standing. Sometimes, I won scholarships for books, and other times, for courses or experiences I wouldn't have been able to afford otherwise.

Each win filled me with gratitude and a sense of accomplishment.

Life was finally starting to change in ways I had never imagined. The crushing weight of financial stress, which had been my constant companion for so long, began to lift. With it came a sense of stability that felt like a dream. Just because things were getting better, my mental health didn't automatically heal. It was still suffering.

With Deepu and our close-knit group of friends, I experienced the joys of college life in ways I never thought I would. They gave me a sense of belonging that I had always longed for. To them, I wasn't "Sushmitha" anymore. I was "Minnu"—the name that I loved slowly returned.

We crammed into the back of a beat-up sedan, six of us laughing and singing along to Bollywood songs on road trips to Cincinnati. The car windows rolled down, and the wind carried our laughter into the air, reminding me of my time with Grandpa on his bicycle and with Daddy on his Vespa. We visited crowded theaters to watch Indian movies, losing ourselves in the familiar colors and drama that reminded us of home. And then there was the trip to Chicago—a sprawling city I had only dreamed of seeing. It was exhilarating to feel so alive, so free.

Three years had passed since I first stepped onto U.S. soil, and while circumstances had kept me from exploring much of the world outside my little circle, that was changing now. Thanks to my friends, I was seeing the world beyond my immediate surroundings, experiencing things I had only ever seen in movies or heard in stories.

I sometimes felt small tagging along, knowing I couldn't contribute much financially. But Deepu—always Deepu—refused to let me feel anything but welcome. She quelled those thoughts with a laugh and a simple truth: to her, I belonged. And that was enough.

Weekends that had once been spent working now became mine for adventures. I finally learned how to drive appropriately and obtained my driver's license, symbolizing independence and freedom.

As the youngest in our group, I was showered with love and affection and treated like a cherished little sibling. It was the first time I truly felt supported and seen.

They celebrated my small wins, comforted me through failures, and reminded me that I was never truly alone. The warmth of their friendship filled gaps I didn't even know existed within me.

Looking back, I realize how much I grew during those college years. The friendships, lessons, and experiences shaped me in ways I could never have predicted. I learned the importance of balance—of working hard but also allowing myself to truly enjoy life. They gifted me stories and memories to cherish and share with my own future children, just as Daddy had once shared his college tales with me.

For me, college was so much more than textbooks and lectures. It was a life-shaping experience. It was where I started to stretch into who I was meant to be—academically, emotionally, socially, and spiritually.

I learned how to make tough decisions and how to handle the consequences. I mastered time management, resolved conflicts, and discovered what it really meant to be independent. I met people from all walks of life, each with their values, and that diversity expanded my world in ways I couldn't have imagined. It taught me empathy, forced me to challenge everything I thought I knew, and opened my mind in ways that forever changed me.

Socially, the college gave me friendships I still treasure. It was where I found my voice, where I learned to speak up, listen, collaborate, and lead. I made mistakes—some big ones. I overslept and missed a final. I chose the wrong paths at times. I trusted the wrong people. But every misstep became a lesson, and slowly, those lessons helped me build the person I am today.

College wasn't just about preparing me for a job; it was about preparing me for life. It marked the beginning of my lifelong journey to understand who I am, what I value, and how I want to present myself.

"Be mature enough to accept rejections and failures."

The Courage to Rise

As the saying goes, all good things must come to an end. Deepu—my friend, sister, and partner in crime—completed her master's degree and had to leave for a job. Her departure marked the end of an era, a chapter of my life filled with warmth and unwavering support.

But what made her leaving even harder was our argument before she left. It was over a silly 'he said/ she said' scenario —something that now feels trivial and silly but at the time felt monumental. That argument, born out of youthful stubbornness and misplaced emotions, shattered something beautiful. And worse, it was irreversible.

I had forgiven people for far greater offenses—those who had hurt me deeply—because I was desperate for love and belonging. Yet here I was, allowing a trivial matter to come between me and the one friend who had loved me unconditionally.

The distance had already settled like an unspoken goodbye when I realized my mistake. Deepu moved to another country, married, and built her own life. The dreams we once clung to—standing beside each other at weddings and celebrating milestones—evaporated. It was a painful lesson in the fragility of relationships and the cost of letting pride interfere with what truly matters.

After Deepu left, I returned to university and completed my bachelor's degree. Soon after, I secured an internship in New York City and packed my life into two suitcases. Moving was easy back then; I owned little but carried a heart full of dreams.

When I first arrived, I stayed with friends from Wright State who had moved there for work after finishing their Master's degree. My new home was a dingy basement in New Jersey, where I lived as a paying guest. It was cramped, damp, and suffocating, but I told myself it was temporary.

At first, I thought my sadness came from my living conditions—the dark, windowless basement, the endless noise of the city above, the loneliness of a place that never truly felt like home.

But soon, the sadness thickened into something heavier—something I couldn't name or escape. Something I couldn't shake.

I was exhausted all the time. My migraines worsened, forcing me onto medications that dulled the pain but also dulled me. My body started betraying me—episodes of fits, moments when I lost control. I didn't understand what was happening.

Then, one night, I took one too many pills. I was found unresponsive in that New Jersey basement.

At the hospital, the doctors told my friends to inform my parents that their daughter might not survive.

Thousands of miles away, my parents received the news. They nearly lost their breath upon hearing it. They sat by the phone, hands shaking, unable to do anything but pray, cry, and wait—just as they had so many times before. Only this time, I wasn't just struggling; I was slipping away.

I later learned that I had been in a coma for three days before I became responsive.

Taking one's own life is never truly a choice—it is the unbearable weight of pain that silences every other option. It is not about wanting to die but about not knowing how to keep living through the suffering. When I overdosed and slipped into that coma, I wasn't thinking about ending my life. I was trying to escape the relentless ache, trying to silence the pain that had become too much to bear.

But waking up after three days in darkness changed something within me. It felt as if life itself had pulled me back, whispering that my story wasn't meant to conclude there. I had been fighting the wrong battle—not against life, but against the wounds I had never allowed myself to heal. In that fragile moment between despair and survival, I realized that maybe, just maybe, I wasn't meant to leave yet.

Recovery wasn't a single instance of clarity. It was slow, messy, and painful.

There were days when the weight of my emotions threatened to crush me completely—when I couldn't imagine ever feeling whole again.

But as winter always gives way to spring, the light returned slowly and steadily. My strength came back, and hope flickered, then grew.

Through it all, my cousin Sravs, who entered my life when I was in a coma, refused to let me drown. She became my pillar—the person I came home to, the heart that understood every silent struggle without judgment. She loved fiercely and unconditionally, as naturally as breathing.

With her beside me, I began to see life anew—not as a force that kept breaking me, but as clay I could reshape. Small kindnesses, sudden bursts of laughter, and the stubborn love of those who stood by me became my reasons to keep going, rebuild, and stay.

The pain had pushed me to the edge, but resilience pulled me back. In that transition, I found something greater than just the will to live; I found the strength to fight for a life that was truly mine.

Once I recovered, I was discharged from the hospital and moved into an apartment with Sravs, who was pursuing her Master's degree, along with a couple of other roommates. Together, we navigated the next phase of our lives—balancing work, studies, and the unpredictable nature of adulthood.

My internship was at a forensics department affiliated with the NYPD, housed in an office on 42nd Street. It was my chance to start over and regain my physical and mental strength.

Every morning, I felt a quiet thrill as I dressed in business attire and stepped into the city's rush, moving with purpose.

The work itself was mostly paperwork—calls, recruiting, and administrative tasks. It wasn't the thrilling fieldwork I had envisioned, but I took it seriously, often staying late to complete everything.

One evening, my boss—a man in his fifties—found me still at my desk late into the night and offered to take me to dinner. Coming from a culture where it's disrespectful to decline an elder's invitation, I obliged.

He took me to a Thai restaurant, where I had the best Singapore noodles of my life. Thin, delicate noodles coated with turmeric and curry powder, paired with shrimp—each bite was a burst of warmth and spice. We talked about each other's families, and he expressed appreciation for my hard work.

I thrive on appreciation. His words encouraged me, making me want to prove myself even more. By the end of the meal, he insisted I take the leftovers home and then dropped me off at the 33rd Street train station in his big black Cadillac Escalade.

The next morning, whispers drifted through the office like smoke. Something felt odd.

A coworker pulled me aside, his voice low and careful. "Just be careful," he said. "The last intern he took to dinner became his baby mama. His wife knows. She doesn't care."

My stomach twisted.

At that moment, the weight of reality hit me like a tidal wave—this man, old enough to be my father, hadn't just been generous. He had intentions. And those intentions sent a cold chill down my spine.

From that day forward, I made myself invisible to him. I avoided eye contact, kept conversations brief and professional, and never allowed myself to be alone in a room with him.

It was a jarring reminder of how easily young women—especially vulnerable ones—can become prey, even in spaces that dress themselves up as "opportunity."

Life after college felt like a tightrope—one misstep, and I could fall. I balanced ambition with survival, carrying the pressure of making something of myself while constantly watching my back.

I celebrated milestones alone. There was no family cheering from the sidelines, only the occasional kindness of friends or strangers—small acts that carried me from one chapter to the next.

But even so, I was learning how to stand—stand—on my own.

Every morning, I rose with a quiet determination. I got ready, walked to the PATH station, took the train to 33rd Street, and then walked again until I reached 42nd. Rain or shine, snow or sun, that routine became my rhythm for eight long months.

The job paid the bills, but it was never the destination.

It was just a pit stop.

I wanted more.

I was waiting to hear back from graduate programs, holding onto hope like a lifeline. When the acceptance letter finally arrived, I stared at it in disbelief.

I had been accepted into a Healthcare program—an opportunity I hadn't dared to imagine was real. It felt like a quiet affirmation that life was still nudging me forward despite all the detours and heartaches.

Without hesitation, I quit my job at the agency and returned to school. Around the same time, my childhood best friend, Rams, moved to the U.S. to pursue her master's degree. She moved in with us, and just like that, our tiny apartment swelled with laughter, shared meals, and the comforting presence of someone who had known me long before any of this began.

Even though the days were long—full of commutes, classes, and late-night assignments—coming home to that warm, noisy, love-filled space made everything bearable.

But my time in New Jersey wasn't always so full. In fact, it had started at the opposite end of the spectrum—quiet, uncertain, and solitary. My living situations mirrored my emotional rollercoaster, which felt like an ECG, with soaring highs and sudden lows.

In the beginning, I stayed in a basement as a paying guest, and that's where the overdose happened.

Later, Sravs, Rams, and I moved into an apartment with two software engineers. They had steady jobs, so we didn't have to worry about money for a while. We celebrated birthdays, hosted friends, and filled that space with love and laughter. I didn't have much to give financially, so I offered what I could—home-cooked meals and a spirit of warmth.

But like so much else, that stability didn't last.

When the roommates moved out, we couldn't afford to stay in the same apartment. My cousin and I had to search for something cheaper, which led us to a cramped attic apartment. The ceiling sloped so low that we couldn't stand upright in parts of the bathroom—we had to sit to shower. The kitchen was communal, shared with strangers who came and went without connection or conversation.

It wasn't ideal, but it was within our means, and we made it work.

As a scholarship student, I was constantly juggling. My academic program was demanding, leaving me little time to work. I was lucky to secure a student ambassador position that helped with rent and expenses, and later, a scholarship from the presidential fund made continuing my education even possible.

Still, there were hard months. Exhausting, anxious, scraping-the-bottom kind of months.

But I wasn't alone. My cousin quietly picked up the slack—bringing groceries when she could. And then there was Krina, a classmate whose kindness I'll never forget. She ran a small side hustle selling handmade chapatis, and each week, she would slip a few into my bag or hands—no fanfare, no fuss.

To her, they were just chapatis. To me, they represented comfort. They symbolized a friend in need. They proved that even when things felt impossibly hard, someone was looking out for me.

And somehow, that made all the difference.

Through the people who touch my life in small and big ways, I learned generosity isn't just about giving—it's about the connection it creates, the way it reminds us that even in our hardest moments, we are not alone. Krina's kindness sustained me in ways she may never fully understand. It wasn't just the food; it was the quiet reassurance that someone cared. That mattered.

Every morning, I woke up to prepare for school. While I was getting ready, I spoke to Mummy and Daddy, chatting about the day. That call assured them that I was safe, so they waited for that call every single day.

When Daddy called one morning and asked if I had thought about marriage, I didn't immediately dismiss it. Maybe it was exhaustion. Maybe it was loneliness. Or perhaps that quiet, unspoken longing—for stability and belonging— made me pause.

I wasn't in a relationship. I had no reason to say no.

So, I agreed to speak with him. Just a conversation, I told myself—a way to see if there was something worth exploring. There were a couple of prospects, but I chose him—Madhu. And if I were being sincere, I chose him because I liked his name better than the other option. It was silly, but sometimes, the smallest details spark something within us.

Daddy passed on my interest to a family friend who had brought the proposal. That evening, my phone rang.

Madhu called me on his way back from the airport after dropping off a friend who was leaving for India. His voice was calm but distant, the weight of farewell still lingering. He wasn't in the best mood but wanted to oblige his family's wishes. I understood that. This wasn't some grand romantic meeting; it was two strangers, connected by tradition and family, cautiously stepping into unknown territory.

Our first conversation was brief. It was formal, a rundown of our lives, where we studied, what we did for work, and what we liked to do. It felt like an interview, but there was something in his voice—a quiet sincerity that made me want to know more. We agreed to speak again.

A few days of phone calls turned into exchanged photos. I studied his picture for longer than I admitted to myself, wondering if this was the face I'd one day wake up to every morning. Before we even met in person, both families decided to move forward.

Neither of us objected.

Madhu was easy to fall for—not because of grand gestures or poetic words, but because of his quiet steadiness. He was handsome, yes, but his kindness drew me in. He reminded me of Daddy.

I had never placed much importance on looks. Daddy had set a different standard for love. He wasn't the tallest or most conventionally attractive man in the room, but he was the best partner Mummy could have asked for—loyal, supportive, and endlessly kind. That was the kind of love I wanted.

And in Madhu, I saw glimpses of that love. *Madhu was also handsome.*

Our courtship was brief—just a handful of in-person meetings and long, winding phone conversations that stretched into the night. With each call, we unraveled small parts of ourselves, revealing just enough to make the other want to know more.

But there were things I hadn't told him yet.

He saw only the surface of who I was then. He didn't know about the past I carried, the wounds that still ached, or the panic attacks that gripped me in the dead of night. Those parts of me would reveal themselves later.

Six months later, we were married.

The wedding took place in India. It was a modest yet deeply heartfelt celebration, funded entirely by my earnings as a student ambassador. There were no extravagant venues or designer outfits, but it was perfect.

My parents, despite the complexities of my adoption, embraced the moment with love and pride.

During the ceremony, as Daddy completed the ritual of giving me away, I saw something I had never seen before – tears in his eyes.

It was a fleeting moment that caught me off guard. Daddy, who always bore the world's weight with unwavering strength, struggled to let me go.

Then Rams, my best friend, stepped forward. She wrapped him in a comforting embrace without hesitation, holding him until he steadied himself.

Mummy, always the quiet pillar of our family, also cried. However, she quickly recovered and poured her love into every wedding detail. She spent countless sleepless nights ensuring everything was perfect within her means.

As the ceremonies concluded, my Nanamma pulled me aside. She looked into my eyes, her hands warm against mine.

"You are fire. Madhu is water. Don't focus on the shortcomings of fire or water. Together, you will create life."

I often marveled at how she understood us so profoundly and so quickly. Perhaps that was the gift of experience. She mentioned that her relationship with my grandfather was similar- a magical dance of opposites that made their marriage last for decades.

Standing beside my husband, family, and friends that day, I realized something profound: happiness isn't found in extravagance. It is found in love, in enduring life's challenges together, and in the quiet belief that if you hold on long enough, your time will come.

"When you change, don't announce it. Just bloom."

Healing in Faith

If you had asked me years ago what it meant to have faith, I would have given you a very different answer. Back then, faith was a ritual, a set of rules I followed out of fear rather than love. I believed in God, but I also thought He was distant—watching from above, keeping score, handing out rewards and punishments. If I prayed, I expected protection. If I suffered, I assumed I had done something to deserve it.

I was wrong.

I grew up in a deeply religious household. My grandmother, Nanamma, was the pillar of our family's faith, devout in her worship of Lord Rama. Every morning, without fail, she performed her prayers with unwavering devotion. I watched her bow before the idols, whispering words with such intensity that it seemed she truly believed she was being heard. Yet, for all her devotion, life had not been kind to her.

She had known great wealth as a child, only to be thrust into hardship as an adult. She buried children, watched her family's fortunes disappear, and endured endless struggles. And still, she prayed.

One day, unable to contain my frustration, I asked her, *"Nanamma, you pray every day. Your prayers, whom did they help? You or your children?"*

She looked at me, not with anger, but with a soft smile. *"You,"* she said. *"You are the blessing God gave me for all my years of devotion."*

I wanted to believe her, but her words only confused me at the time. If faith was meant to bring blessings, why was there still suffering? If God loved us, why did He allow pain?

I clung to Nanamma's rituals, but they felt like duties—not comfort. I prayed because I feared what would happen if I didn't. I believed every hardship I faced was a punishment for some unknown sin. At fourteen, when I endured hunger, abuse, and loss, I asked, What did I do to deserve this? I begged for relief, for signs, for answers.

While grappling with faith, I didn't find Jesus—He found me. It wasn't in a church or through a grand revelation. It arrived quietly, like a whisper stitched into my soul.

Faith did come as a sudden miracle into my life. But as I dove deep into faith, I realized that God had been walking beside me all along. He was there on the nights I cried myself to sleep, thinking no one heard me. He was there in the hands that lifted me when I had fallen.

And in that realization, everything changed.

For the first time, I saw God not as a punishing force but as a loving presence. He wasn't waiting for perfection or watching me struggle for sport.

He was simply *with me*.

Faith gave me what rituals never could—peace. It freed me from the guilt and fear I had carried for so long. It taught me that suffering was not a punishment but a part of life and that God didn't promise a life without trials. He promised that I would never have to walk through them alone.

Faith didn't erase my pain, but it helped me face it. It softened the bitterness in my heart and replaced it with something greater—hope.

Faith gave me the courage to forgive and the wisdom to be grateful. It led me toward joy, but more than that, it revealed one of the greatest lessons of all—kindness is faith in action.

For so long, I believed that kindness was about receiving something in return and that helping others should bring gratitude or recognition.

But faith taught me otherwise. Genuine kindness isn't transactional – it's transformational. It changes not just the one who receives it but also the one who gives it.

I think back to the moments when kindness saved me: the strangers who offered me food when I had nothing, the teachers who saw potential in me when I felt invisible, and the friends who simply listened when I had no words left. They may never know how deeply their kindness shaped my life.

But I know. They acted as a tangible form of God.

And because of them, I choose to pass that kindness on—not for praise or validation, but because I understand what it feels like to be lost in the darkness, searching for even the smallest flicker of light.

If faith has taught me anything, we are meant to be that light for one another.

Wherever you are in your journey, I want you to know this: Faith isn't about having all the answers. It isn't about being perfect. It isn't about *finding* God—because He has already found you.

Faith is about trust.

It's about taking the next step, even when the path is unclear.

It's about choosing love over fear, hope over despair.

And most importantly, it's about never believing the lie that you are alone.

So tonight, as you lay your head down, take a deep breath.

Let go of the guilt, fear, and need to figure it all out.

Whisper a prayer, not because you have to, but because you *can*.

And know that God is right there with you at that moment, as He always has been.

"Fight all your battles with prayer; you will always win."

Letting Go

There are moments when pain settles so deeply inside us that it feels like a permanent part of who we are. Wounds we never asked for. Hurts we never deserved. And yet, we carry them as if letting go would erase what happened—as if our pain is the only proof it was real.

I believed that once.

I thought if I held onto my anger—clung to every betrayal—I'd never feel powerless again.

That rage led me to strive, never to give up, and became my armor. But it didn't protect me. It caged me.

Forgiveness once felt like weakness—too soft for the pain this sharp.

And some wounds don't fade with time. They linger, just beneath the surface, waiting to be reopened by a word, a memory, a silence.

I lived with that pain for years—nights spent replaying betrayals, wishing I could rewrite the past.

The ones who hurt me—those who should've protected me—left scars I still feel.

The sponsoring parents promised a better life and gave me something worse.

The nights that took what could never be returned.

The guardian who made me feel invisible.

The sibling who twisted love into fear.

My parents, who loved me, couldn't see the danger closing in.

How do you forgive that? How do you release what's rooted so deep?

There was no epiphany, just a slow, painful chipping away.

What I realized, rather slowly, was that they weren't the ones suffering under the weight of my pain; I was.

My breath caught, my chest tightened, and my mind spiraled when their names came up. I was still letting them hold power.

That's when I realized—I deserved peace. But I didn't know how to obtain it.

And if forgiving them felt impossible, forgiving myself was even harder. For what I didn't see. For staying silent. For trusting the wrong people. For every choice, I regretted—like losing $5,000 to a scam in a desperate attempt to build a future.

I shamed myself endlessly. I would think—if a friend told me this story, would I call them foolish?

No. I'd hold them. I'd say, "You did what you had to. You were trying to survive."

If I could offer grace to others, why not myself? I didn't have an answer to that question.

Then I heard the story—the moment Jesus, bloodied and broken, looked into the eyes of those who mocked, tortured, and crucified him… and said, *"Father, forgive them, for they do not know what they are doing."*

And something inside me cracked open.

How could he do that? How could he ask for mercy for the very people stripping him of his dignity—as they were doing it? There was no apology, no remorse, no justice—just pain. And still… he chose forgiveness.

I sat with that.

Even though I wasn't nailed to a cross, I knew what it meant to be wounded by people who should have protected me, to be hurt without apology, to carry the weight of injustice, and to feel like forgiveness was a betrayal.

At that moment, I realized something profound: forgiveness isn't a weakness. It's not surrender to those who harmed you.

It's the ultimate reclaiming of power.

It's saying, *You don't get to shape who I become.*

That story didn't erase my pain, but it gave me a new way to carry it—not as armor or rage but as something sacred—a chance to live beyond what was done to me.

And from that point on, I began to change.

Letting go didn't happen all at once. Some days, anger still rises. Some days, that voice whispers, "You weren't enough." But now I know it's just an old wound. That is not the truth.

Forgiveness isn't a single act —it's a daily reckoning—a quiet, deliberate choice to loosen the grip on what has already hurt you enough.

And here's what I've come to understand:

You can't hate yourself into healing. You can't bloom in soil soaked with self-blame.

For years, I was stuck—replaying the past, drowning in shame convinced my pain was proof of who I was. But how could I ever become the woman I longed to be if I kept cutting her down?

So, I chose differently.

I chose to grow. To forgive—not just them, but myself. To believe I was worth saving.

Some weights were never meant to follow us into the future and I began to set down what was never mine to carry.

It was never about them.

It was about finding the parts of me buried beneath the hurt. About rising and saying, *This ends with me.*

So, if you're carrying something heavy—if your heart feels worn from holding on—please hear this:

You don't have to release it all today. You don't have to forgive right now.

But when the time comes—and you choose peace over pain—you will feel something shift.

Not because the past stops mattering or hurting. But because *you* deserve it.

You deserve peace and rest.

"Remember, when you forgive, you heal.
And when you let go, you grow."

The Secret Ingredient

When life is falling apart, your heart feels heavy, and everything seems to be working against you, hearing someone tell you to *just be grateful*" can feel like an insult.

Gratitude? For what? The sleepless nights? The heartbreak? The feeling of being stuck while everyone else seems to be moving forward?

I get it.

There were nights when I lay awake in a house that didn't feel like home, staring at the ceiling, wondering how my life had turned out this way. Nights when hunger gnawed at my stomach, but loneliness gnawed even deeper. Times when I felt invisible, unheard, and utterly alone.

And in those moments, gratitude felt impossible.

I wasn't ungrateful—I was just exhausted. I was tired of fighting, hoping, and watching the world move on while I felt frozen in place. People would say, "Things will get better." But what if they didn't?

It's hard to be grateful when all you feel is empty.

But here's what I've learned: gratitude is not about pretending life is perfect. It's not about ignoring pain or forcing yourself to smile when you feel like falling apart.

When you're in pain, don't rush past it. Let yourself feel it—fully, deeply. Don't bury it. Speak it aloud to someone who will listen. Cry if tears come. Rest when you're weary. Pray if it brings you peace. Reach out; you don't have to carry it alone.

Only after you've honored your grief, your anger, and your exhaustion—"only then" can you begin to take small steps toward gratitude.

You can't force thankfulness over unhealed wounds. Suppressed pain will always whisper beneath the surface, stealing the joy you try to claim. "True gratitude grows from soil that's been tended, not skipped over."

So tend to your heart first. Then, when you're ready, let the light in—slowly, gently, one small grace at a time.

Gratitude is about noticing.

Start noticing the small, quiet moments of good. Notice what remains, even after so much has been lost. That one subtle shift in perspective? It can change everything.

For years, the kindness of strangers I wrote about in this book faded from my memory. But gratitude doesn't demand grand gestures. If it feels impossible now, start small.

I began by whispering: 'It was hard, but thank God I survived. Thank God I was carried through.'

You don't have to force thankfulness for the heartbreak or the struggle—no one asks that of you. But can you find one thing, however slight, that brings comfort?

Maybe it's the warmth of your morning coffee, the way sunlight spills across the floor, or a song that unexpectedly tugs at your heart—proof, even now, that you can still feel.

Sometimes, light seeps in through the cracks we didn't even know were there. Maybe it's a friend who checks in, even if you don't always respond.

Perhaps it's the simple fact that, despite everything, you're still here.

These moments don't erase the pain but remind you that life isn't only pain. Even in chaos, beauty still exists. And when you start to notice it, something shifts.

Because gratitude isn't about being naive; it's about survival. It's about anchoring yourself to the good so the bad doesn't pull you under.

For so long, I believed my life was defined by what I lacked—the love I never received, the stability I never had, the people who let me down.

But gratitude changed that.

It didn't rewrite my past but gave me a new way to see it.

Yes, I lost things. But I also gained things.

I gained resilience, independence, and the kindness of strangers who stepped in when my family failed me. I gained lifelong friends. I gained a better version of myself despite my past.

And when I focused on what I had instead of what I lost, my entire story changed.

So, how do you make gratitude a part of your life?

Start small.

Write down three things you're grateful for every day. Even if it's just, I woke up today. I have a roof over my head. I heard a song I love.

Say thank you out loud, even if it's just to the space around you.

Tell the people in your life that you appreciate them.

And when challenges come, instead of asking Why me? Try asking What can this teach me?

It doesn't mean you have to love the struggle. But it helps you make meaning out of it.

If I had waited for life to be perfect before practicing gratitude, I'd still be waiting.

Instead, I started where I was, with what I had.

And what I had—though it didn't seem like much at the time—was enough to keep me going.

And that's what I want for you.

Gratitude won't fix everything overnight. But it will change how you see the world. And sometimes, that's enough.

So tonight, before you go to bed, say a quiet prayer and pause.

Take a deep breath.

Find one thing—just one—to be grateful for.

Then do it again tomorrow. And watch how it changes you.

Because one day, you'll look back and realize that gratitude didn't just shift your mindset.

It changed you. It makes your life colorful.

"Be grateful for every single stage of your life."

Conclusion

As I reach the final pages of this story, I want to pause—not just to reflect but to honor you, the reader, for walking this path with me. You have carried these moments alongside me and felt the weight of the darkness.

I began this story as Minnu—a spark, a flicker of light in the shadows of uncertainty. That light was dimmed and many times left in a full-blown wind, but somehow, that light never went out. It grew, even in the dark.

Yes, life dealt me hardships beyond my control. But the truth is, I wasn't just a passive victim of my story. My choices—how I responded, how I carried pain, how I kept walking—shaped the path as much as the pain itself.

As you read, there was a time when hunger was my closest companion, and I wondered where my next meal would come from. Food was not just nourishment but power, permission, and a symbol of love withheld.

I needed to heal to emerge from this alive. But true healing, contrary to my expectations, didn't come from outside. It began the moment I turned inward—when I stopped waiting for someone else to save me and realized that strength, courage, and resilience had been within me all along.

With that healing, I opened my home freely and shared my table without hesitation. In that simple act, I reclaimed something deeper than control—I reclaimed my power.

I walked away from places that diminished me. I left abuse behind, even when it felt like all I had ever known. I kept moving forward, even when the road disappeared beneath my feet. In that journey, I found something greater than healing.

I found freedom.

I wish the sponsoring parents who planted the seeds for our journey to the U.S. had done so with love, patience, and a steady heart. I wish good intentions had guided their decision and I wish they had the emotional strength to see it through. I wish they had recognized their limits—how much they could take on without unraveling under the weight of it.

I wish it hadn't ended the way it did—so abruptly, under such painful circumstances. I wish there had been space for understanding, for grace. I wish I could still have a relationship with them—one rooted in gratitude for the opportunity they gave me instead of the silence that now stands in its place.

I grieve that I couldn't become the daughter my adoptive parents hoped for.

As a mother, I now understand the kind of love a child brings into your life—the joy that no person or thing can replace. I see what they must have longed for, and I understand now what they might have hoped to feel in my presence.

But the journey left scars too deep to ignore. To truly heal, I made the painful decision to sever ties. It was the only way I knew to move forward. And yet, I still wish the story had been different.

I wish I had been there to care for them in their old age. I wish I had stood by my adoptive father when he took his last breath. I wish I could now offer my adoptive mother the comfort and care she deserves.

But in this lifetime, in this story—that is not how it ends.

Does abuse make you bitter?

It can. It can harden you, wrap its hands around your heart, and squeeze until all that's left is resentment. It can whisper that survival means becoming the very thing that hurt you.

But I chose differently. I chose to break the cycle.

My abusers, too, were once victims—shaped by the cruelty they later passed on. They followed the pattern, passing down pain as an inheritance.

And now, I stand at the same crossroads with the same choice.

To repeat what was done to me—or rise above it. To let my wounds become weapons—or heal them, so they never cut another soul. To surrender to the darkness—or reach for the light.

That choice isn't easy. It takes more than will—it takes work, courage, and the painful process of unlearning what was ingrained, of choosing the unknown over the familiar, of rewriting the script and standing against the tide of generational pain to say: *It ends with me.*

True strength isn't just surviving suffering—it's ending it not just for yourself but for those who come after you. It's choosing love where you were unloved. Kindness where you were broken. It's turning toward yourself with grace.

Our past does not define us—our choices do. We are not bound by what has hurt us but by how we rise from it.

No matter where you come from or how impossible your circumstances may seem, you are not defined by your struggles. Your resilience determines you. By the love you give. By the kindness you choose, even when the world hasn't been kind to you.

And part of that kindness? It's the grace you extend to yourself.

Closure doesn't come from perfect endings; it comes from peace. It comes from learning to live with unanswered questions, from being okay with no confrontation and no apology, and from understanding that healing isn't about fixing the past—It's about making peace with it.

If there is one thing I want you to take from my story, it's this:

Keep going.

Fight for your voice. Fight for your dreams. Fight for the life you were meant to live.

Surround yourself with those who lift you. And when you find light—do not hoard it. **Please pass it on.**

I have always been strong. Strength was woven into me long before I knew its name. I watched Mummy and my grandmothers—women who bore their burdens with quiet resilience. Strength lived in their hands, in their sacrifices, in the way they kept going without fanfare.

When life tested me and pushed me to the very edge, that strength surfaced again. Not just to survive but to transform.

Moving to the United States forced that strength to evolve. Making decisions alone and navigating indifference taught me that true strength is not about holding on but knowing when to let go. It's about choosing kindness when life has been cruel. It's about forgiving—not because someone deserves it but because pain becomes too heavy to carry. It's about lifting others, even when it's inconvenient.

No one should have to suffer to learn resilience. Strength shouldn't be earned through hardship. I do not wish my path on anyone. But I refuse to define my life based on what it took from me.

Instead, I define it by who I became.

Your strength is already within you.

You do not need to lose yourself to find it. You do not need to suffer to prove it. Strength is not about never falling—it's about rising again, even when it seems impossible. It is about knowing your worth, even when others fail to see it.

If life has tested you, let it teach you. But don't let it define you. Carry your strength forward not as a weapon but as a light—for yourself and others.

Kindness isn't a grand gesture. It's a warm meal when someone is hungry, a safe space when someone is afraid, and a single word that says: **You matter.**

If you are in a position to guide or protect a young person, take it seriously. Speak life into them. Show them that their dreams are worth chasing. Be the person you once needed—or the person you were lucky to have.

And to those who are struggling right now, who wonder if they will ever make it through—

Know this: your story is not over. The best chapters are still ahead.

Keep writing. Keep believing.

When you find your way, never forget to turn around and offer a hand to someone still searching.

Because, in the end, that is what truly matters.

Minnu never disappeared. She just waited quietly and patiently until I was strong enough to carry both names, both lives. And now I have them both with pride.

With love and hope,

Minnu

Some will see you as brave; others will call you a coward.

To some, you will be strong; to others, fragile.

One person will think you are kind,

while another will say you are cruel.

Your presence may bring comfort to some,

while making others uneasy.

No matter what you do,

people will see you differently.

They will not agree; they never do.

So why live for their opinions?

Live life on your own terms.

Find happiness—the kind that comes from within.

The truest joy lies in giving,

in caring for others,

in making someone feel seen, heard, and loved.

Be okay with being misunderstood.

Not everyone will see your heart,

and not everyone will know your truth.

And that is okay.

Find solace in faith.

Let His love fill the empty spaces,

His grace steady you when the world is unsteady,

And his light guide you when the path is unclear.

But as you live, be kind-
to yourself, to others, to the world around you.
Do no harm—not to your heart, not to theirs,
not to the earth that holds us all.

Let go of what they think.
Live in a way that feels true to you.

And through it all, no matter what comes,
stand tall, stay true—
Unbroken.